Praise for *A Compelling Faith in a Compromising Culture*

If you watch the news even for a few minutes or scroll through your Instagram feed, you'll see arguments, protests, and downright hate thrown around everywhere! So how are we as Christians supposed to live when the larger culture around us is quick to make compromises? I'm thankful to my friend Mike for addressing this very question in his new book. It's not about fighting back against culture, and it's not about going quiet either. Instead, as Jesus followers, we're called to be deeply rooted in what we know is true. Searching for calm in the chaos like so many of us are? Don't miss the wisdom Mike has to share!

Adam Weber, lead pastor of Embrace Church, podcaster, author

My good friend Mike Tatlock has written a book "for such a time as this." *A Compelling Faith in a Compromising Culture* reflects Mike's years of ministering here in Portland, Oregon, a city that's been at the epicenter of so many of the cultural tensions facing our nation. There are time-proven ways that we, as the church, and as individual followers of Jesus, can work for the shalom of our cities and neighborhoods without compromising biblical truth. Anyone burdened by the season we're in and looking for practical ways forward needs to read this book.

Kevin Palau, CEO, Palau

As a fellow pastor and leadership coach, I found *A Compelling Faith in a Compromising Culture* to be one of the most timely and transformative books I have read in years. Mike Tatlock speaks directly to the pressures leaders and believers are facing in today's cultural climate, offering not only a clear diagnosis of the moment we are living in but also deep and practical biblical solutions. His insights into rootedness, identity, and spiritual resilience are pastorally wise and prophetically bold. This book strengthens the heart, sharpens conviction, and calls the church back to a faith that stands firm, shines brightly, and engages the world with courage and compassion. It is a message every Christian and every leader needs right now.

Benjamin Lundquist, Pastoral Coaching and Leadership Development; host of the *Rise and Lead Podcast*

My friend Mike Tatlock has always been a model for how to be a Christian on mission in a context of hostility and compromise. I've seen his ministry in the flesh—and he has modeled what it means to live faithfully in a cultural context swirling with difficulty, chaos, and pain. This book is a testimony to that fruitful ministry. And it is a gift to the church as he is sharing his secrets for faithfulness. I commend this. And hope you find it a helping hand from an elder brother ahead.

A.J. Swoboda, associate professor of Bible and Theology at Bushnell University; author of *A Teachable Spirit*

Mike Tatlock is a pastor who combines an all-in heart, a deep wisdom for living a disciple's life, and riveting writing. He brings deep biblical and pastor insight to lead readers to *A Compelling Faith in a Compromising Culture*. Enjoy his author skills and grow to the joy of the life of a Jesus follower.

Gerry Breshears, Professor of Theology, Western Seminary

Mike is a master at keeping faith practical, and this is proof. "Deep yet simple" is how I describe the content. Follow his lead through this journey and you just might discover a freedom you never knew existed.

Chuck Bomar, entrepreneur, author, and President & COO, Barna Group

A COMPELLING FAITH IN A COMPROMISING CULTURE

Mike Tatlock

MOODY PUBLISHERS
CHICAGO

Edited by David Burnette
Cover design: Graham Terry

ISBN: 978-0-8024-3468-5

Originally delivered by fleets of horse-drawn wagons, the affordable paperbacks from D. L. Moody's publishing house resourced the church and served everyday people. Now, after more than 125 years of publishing and ministry, Moody Publishers' mission remains the same—even if our delivery systems have changed a bit. For more information on other books (and resources) created from a biblical perspective, go to www.moodypublishers.com or write to:

Moody Publishers
820 N. LaSalle Boulevard
Chicago, IL 60610

1 3 5 7 9 10 8 6 4 2

Printed in the United States of America

To my wife, Bernadette, you are the steady grace beside me, the rock of our home, and the anchor that has kept me through every storm. Your love is the quiet strength behind these pages, and your faith is the unseen thread woven through them.

To Jadon and Mikiah, you are the living reminders that God's promises are true. Your lives inspire me to live for Jesus, love deeper, and keep pressing into the Father's heart.

To my mother, Diana, your prayers have built foundations I now stand on, and your love has been a shelter in every season. I am the fruit of your faith, and this book is in many ways a reflection of the seeds you faithfully sowed.

You've all taught me that the best chapters in life aren't written on paper, but lived with you.

Contents

Introduction *9*

1 Contending: Fighting the Good Fight *19*

2 Heart Check: The Choice of Allegiance *37*

3 Consecration: Purging the Idols from Our Lives *53*

4 Beyond Consumption: Feasting on the Goodness of God *63*

5 Increasing Capacity: The Power of Pausing *73*

6 Identity Issues: God Says Who We Are *85*

7 Count the Cost: Loosening the Grip on Self *99*

8 Radical Character: The Joy of Persevering *111*

9 Fearless Engagement: Don't Be Scared of the World *129*

10 Radical Community: The Power of Proximity *141*

Epilogue *153*

Notes *157*

Introduction
Strong in the Storm

Recently, I returned from officiating a destination wedding in the Caribbean (rough assignment, I know). As our flight made its final descent to the Cancun airport, the pilot calmly informed us that we would be landing in a tropical storm. You could sense the tension in the cabin. Bodies bolted upright. Eyes widened. Fingers tightened around armrests. This landing had the potential to be bumpy—and it was.

Instead of descending gently, the aircraft dropped suddenly into air pockets—then trembled before stabilizing. Gusts of horizontal rain and wind pelted the fuselage. Thankfully, the pilot managed to straighten the wings before touching down on the tarmac. You could almost hear the passengers collectively exhale.

But the storm was still raging. Walking outside the terminal ushered us into a powerful display of the forces of nature. Lightning, thunder, and a torrential downpour combined with howling winds that threatened to uproot every tree in the rainforest canopy. A few branches broke free, but the trees didn't fall. The palm trees were especially impressive. They took the full brunt of the violent winds without breaking. Amid such a barrage, the massive Douglas Firs, so numerous in the Pacific Northwest where I live, would have fallen with a mighty crash. But the palm trees were built differently. They bend, but don't break. They have long roots that extend deep into the earth. What happened beneath the soil enabled them to withstand what happened above the surface.

Standing in the Storm

I couldn't help but think it was a great picture of how Christians can remain steadfast in the current cultural storm. Make no mistake: We are in a storm. Perhaps you already feel it. Whether it's the influence of ideologies and philosophies such as postmodernism, or the popular assumption that you should be "true to yourself," belief in basic Christian doctrines continues to be eroded. Christian teachings on family and sexuality, once respected by the wider culture, are now considered suspect or downright dangerous. Gone are the days when Christians could expect to be respected in the eyes of secular institutions and given inroads into broader society. Increasingly, the Western world finds the church unnecessary, offensive, and irrelevant. The storm continues to move Christians from the center of society to the margins. This shift has left many of us feeling disoriented and discouraged.

Some believe the answer is to fight the storm. To rally our troops and push back against the onslaught. With enough organization, activism, and legislation, we can beat back the forces arrayed against us and recapture the respect we once commanded.

Others want to hide. Batten down the hatches and ride out the storm. The culture is beyond hope, they reason. Let's disengage and isolate. The best we can hope to do is protect ourselves.

But there's a third way, and it's the one I believe God is calling us to. It prescribes neither war nor surrender. Instead, it's all about roots.

If we want an unshakable faith, one that not only withstands the storm but produces fruit, then we must determine where our faith is rooted. Listen to what the prophet Jeremiah says about the importance of roots:

> But blessed is the one who trusts in the LORD,
> whose confidence is in him.
> They will be like a tree planted by the water
> that sends out its roots by the stream.
> It does not fear when heat comes;
> its leaves are always green.
> It has no worries in a year of drought
> and never fails to bear fruit. (Jer. 17:7–8)

Confidence to withstand external pressures is directly connected to trusting in the Lord and being rooted in Him.

The Christian life is like an organism: it needs nourishment to grow healthy and remain strong. It starts with a tiny seed of faith planted by God in the soil of our hearts. Growth in the Chrisitan life is similar to the growth of a seed. As the seed begins to grow into a plant, it pushes up *and* down. As the first leaves poke through the soil, roots stretch down into the earth to sustain its growth. Likewise, Paul reminded the Colossian church that they needed to be "rooted and built up" in Christ (Col. 2:7).

When our faith is challenged, the best response isn't to push back. It's to go deeper.

Radical Remnant

Going deeper in your faith doesn't sound like enough of a response, but it's actually more radical than you might realize. When you think of the word "radical," what comes to mind? If politics is your thing, it might be an image of a person from the far right or left. What images spring into your brain when you think of a radical Christian? An obnoxious, judgmental guy with a bullhorn on the street corner? Or maybe it's the image of a tacky sticker plastered on the bumper of a vintage Ford Pinto that reads, "This car is prayer conditioned" or "Read the Bible; it will scare the hell out of you." Let me assure you: This is not what Jesus had in mind for His followers. He wanted them to be radical, but not in the way we typically think of the word.

The English word "radical" comes from the Latin word *radicalis,* which has to do with roots. In other words, *radicalis* was all about roots and sustaining life. Sometimes we think being faithful requires being extreme. But it's more about being radical in the original sense of the word: rooted, connected to life. Radical faith is a resilient faith because it's deeply rooted. It can withstand the storm.

One challenge for those who remain rooted amid a shifting culture is that they are often in the minority. This brings us to another "r" word: remnant. The word simply refers to a smaller portion left over from a larger portion or piece. It doesn't only apply to food or material from which a garment is fashioned; it often designates a group of people. Throughout Scripture, God assigned a high value to those of His people, whether past, present, or future, whom He had set aside for holy purposes. These faithful followers who didn't blow away with the winds of persecution and temptation but remained steadfast in their faith.

Jesus made it clear that this remnant would be small. "Many" will find the way to eternal destruction, Jesus warned, but "few" will find the way to eternal life (Matt. 7:13–14). In Scripture, the remnant serves a clear purpose. It is instrumental in preserving God's witness in the world, even in the darkest times. Those who make up the remnant represent the hope, the promise, and the possibility of restoration.

God's Invincible Purposes

The beautiful thing about God's plan is that His desire will be accomplished despite everything that we see happening around us. We are called to serve and glorify God regardless of what transpires in our time. I understand why we're tempted to despair. When I feel discouragement creeping in, I think back to the origins of the church.

The first century church had a very small footprint in the world. It possessed no famous history, heroic resume, or saintly memorials. There were no church buildings (early Christians met in homes). It had not yet established a corpus of great literature or art. The church was still in its infancy. Christians, known first as those belonging to "the Way" (Acts 9:2), consisted of a few obscure, marginalized communities scattered over the Roman Empire. It was composed mostly of the humblest members of society: slaves, freedmen, and poor artisans. They knew the power of the gospel was more than winning culture wars; it was about winning hearts, redeeming the lost, and overturning the powers of darkness. Culture wars come and go, but the gospel transforms lives.

As a prisoner in Rome, you could hardly blame Paul for lacking enthusiasm about the church's destiny, yet he wrote in cosmic terms about the church, knowing its paltry presence would result in an eternal glory: "And God placed all things under his [Christ's] feet and appointed him to be head over everything for the church, which is his body, the fullness of him who fills everything in every way" (Eph. 1:22–23).

You can imagine how these letters lifted those fledging congregations. Paul saw them infused with divine energy, set apart for eternal glory, radiating with heavenly beauty. All the world and its greatness are dwarfed by the church's splendor. They are marked out to have eternal influence.

The gospel they proclaim is the only hope for the nations. The overcoming triumph of Christ finds in them a liberating expression; they are the instrument of Christ's ongoing mission and the possessors of His own Spirit until He returns!

That grand vision of the church is just as true today. Jesus is still calling out a remnant, unmoved by the world, and deeply rooted in Him.

Would There Be Enough Evidence?

Christians with a deeply rooted faith are more likely to be a compelling witness. So how are you doing in this regard? Is your confidence in God evident to those around you? If you were arrested for being a Christian, would there be enough evidence to convict you?

It's a question that stings because it demands more than intellectual belief—it demands wholehearted commitment. In an age where faith is often privatized, reduced to sentiment or slogans, this question drags our spirituality out into the open. It refuses to let Christianity be something merely internal, intellectual, or invisible. It asks: Does your life preach the gospel even when your mouth is shut?

We live in a culture where the highest values are comfort, convenience, and image management. We're praised for tolerance, not truth; for performance, not perseverance; for self-expression, not self-sacrifice. In such a world, a quiet, non-disruptive Christianity fits in just fine, but it also vanishes into irrelevance.

The early church didn't grow because it was safe or silent. It grew because its people lived lives that stood out, marked by compassion for the outcast, sexual purity in a world of indulgence, generosity that broke economic norms, and fearless witness in the face of persecution. They were unmistakable. Arrestable. Convictable.

A compelling faith is one that cannot stay hidden; it shows up in costly love, inconvenient obedience, courageous truth-telling, and a holiness that haunts the status quo. It doesn't just blend in; it bears witness. And that kind of witness always leaves a trail of grace, justice, humility, and the unmistakable aroma of Christ.

The world is aching for something real. Not perfect. Not performative. But prophetic. And our witness is still most compelling when we proclaim the truth and live it out.

In the pages ahead, we will explore how we can press into that high and holy calling. We're going to look at how being members of a remnant affects our identity, our appetites, our behavior, and the way we relate to God and each other. We'll see how every aspect of our lives can be rooted in God's purpose for us at this unique time in history.

I also hope this book will lift your eyes above the current challenges we face and help you glimpse our ultimate purpose in God's sweeping, cosmic plan. It can be tempting to focus on grim headlines and negative cultural developments. But I hope when you close this book, you'll be inspired to keep following hard after God, trusting that He will work in and through our lives. My prayer is that you'll keep shining as a part of the remnant God has preserved for this time.

I know you want to stand strong when the storm winds blow. You don't want to see your fruit dried up by hard circumstances. You don't want to fall. But the storm will only grow stronger, and the only way to ensure you'll endure it is to send your roots down deep. If you are rooted in Christ, the trials and troubles of the world won't move you. You will stand firm, no matter the circumstances.

1

Contending: Fighting the Good Fight

Contending for the faith is not being contentious, it's being courageous.

– JACKIE HILL PERRY

Jamie was a thirty-four-year-old Christian woman who grew up in church, led worship in youth group, and even went on short-term mission trips. But by the time she hit college, something shifted. Her faith wasn't gone; it was just . . . blurred. Replaced, quietly, by a new kind of religion, curated to blend in. She didn't walk away from Jesus. She just drifted, scroll by scroll, post by post, lie by lie.

"You are your image."

"If your life isn't impressive, it's irrelevant."

"Success means visibility."

"Don't offend anyone. Be spiritual, but not too Christian."

She didn't believe those lies outright. But they were whispered daily through reels, influencers, and likes. And slowly, her once bold faith became soft, safe, and silent. Until one day, in a coffee shop, a friend asked her a simple question.

"When is the last time you said Jesus' name out loud?"

The truth hit like a gut-punch. She couldn't remember. She'd become a professional Christian in hiding, shaped more by TikTok algorithms than the Word of God.

Logan was twenty-eight, sharp, creative, and successful. He worked in tech, led a men's group at church, and kept up a solid gym schedule. From the outside, everything looked strong. But underneath, a war was raging. It wasn't drugs or infidelity. It was subtle. Quiet. Almost invisible. It started with compromises that didn't feel like compromises. Scrolling late at night. A little more time on Reddit. A few episodes deeper into Netflix's latest edgy series.

The Word of God slowly got replaced with podcasts and productivity hacks. His prayer life became bullet points. Worship became background noise. Then came the lies, the kind that don't shout, but drip into your spirit like poison:

"You don't need to be that intense."

"Nobody's really living sold out for Jesus anymore."

"Don't be that guy. Just be chill, spiritual-ish."

"Holiness is optional. Grace covers everything."

Logan didn't walk away from Jesus. He just got numb. Then one night, at 2 a.m., after a mindless scroll session and a heavy feeling in his chest, he felt the Holy Spirit press on him: "You've made peace with the enemy's lies."

He realized he hadn't denied Jesus, but he'd stopped fighting for Him.

Elijah was a rising star in the worship scene. His voice was rich. His songs were poetic. He was getting invited to conferences, writing music that blended theology and relevance. Well, kind of. There was more relevance than theology lately.

People loved him because he was "safe." He didn't say hard things. His lyrics were ambiguous enough to work in both Christian and secular circles. He called it "bridge-building." Deep down, though, he was just scared to be clear. He had started editing truth, not with scissors, but with silence.

He wrote songs about love, but never mentioned repentance. He talked about grace, but never about sin. He posted about mental health, injustice, and kindness, but never the name of Jesus. Because that name divides.

One day, he was in LA recording in a studio when a secular artist he admired turned to him and said, "Man, your stuff feels spiritual but not religious. Like, it's vague enough to mean anything. That's what I love about it; it's God without the guilt."

Elijah smiled. But inside, something snapped. He had written songs that inspired everyone but saved no one. He'd become fluent in a language of light with no fire, beauty with no backbone, faith with no foundation.

Maybe you can identify with Elijah or Logan or Jamie. You've been influenced by the world without even realizing it. It's a good reminder that the greatest threat to the church isn't always intense persecution. Sometimes it's gradual persuasion.

The Need to Contend

The greatest threat to the church is not being burned at the stake; it's being slowly boiled in comfort. Satan's goal isn't to scare you out of your faith; it's to lull you into compromise so subtly that you won't even notice you've surrendered.

The opposite of compromise is contending. Not the kind of contending that lashes out in retaliation against the culture, but rather the kind of contending that is fueled by a deep commitment to Christ and His Word. Contending is the tenacity to never cave in regardless of the opposition.

SATAN'S GOAL ISN'T TO SCARE YOU OUT OF YOUR FAITH; IT'S TO LULL YOU INTO COMPROMISE SO SUBTLY THAT YOU WON'T EVEN NOTICE YOU'VE SURRENDERED.

Here's how Jude uses the concept of contending: "Dear friends, although I was very eager to write to you about the salvation we share, I felt compelled to write and urge you to contend for the faith that was once for all entrusted to God's holy people" (Jude 1:3).

The book of Jude is a short but powerful letter written to early Christians. It was written because their faith was under siege from false teachers. This admonition to contend refers to an intense effort. A wrestling match gives a vivid picture of contending, as there is an ongoing struggle to maintain control over an opponent. Neither participant is willing to give up until the other is clearly pinned or defeated.

Jude was not writing to believers to help them feel content, but to help them be vigilant. Having assured them of the love of God and His unsurpassed power to keep them safe (Jude 1), Jude next shows believers the danger that surrounds them. And he tells them to fight for the faith.

The best argument for the faith is when the remnant live it.

The Battle Is Spiritual

If we want to effectively contend for the faith, we need to know what kind of war we're in. Ultimately, our battle is spiritual. Satan is trying to take you down and keep you from doing God's will. He attacks you with busyness, exhaustion, guilt, addiction, or whatever else he can think of. He wants to keep you fighting the things you can see, like the people around you, rather than the true enemy.

Spiritual warfare is the struggle against evil forces that seek to thwart God's purposes and harm His people. Ephesians 6:12 says, "For our struggle is not against flesh and blood, but against the rulers, against the authorities, against the powers of this dark world and against the spiritual forces of evil in the heavenly realms." Our true enemies are not human, but spiritual beings orchestrating sin and rebellion against God.

Even though spiritual warfare runs through both the Old and New Testaments, the apostle Paul helps identify the three main aspects of spiritual warfare: the world, the flesh, and the devil. Here's how he described it to the church at Ephesus:

> You were dead in the trespasses and sins in which you once walked, following the course of this world, following the prince of the power of the air, the spirit that is now at work in the sons of disobedience—among whom we all once lived in the passions of our flesh, carrying out the desires of the flesh and the mind, and were by nature children of wrath, like the rest of mankind. (Eph. 2:1–3 ESV)

The world

The world represents people, religions, governments, or worldly systems that oppose Christ. The world that rejects the truth of Christ is under the control, or deception, of the god of this world (2 Cor. 4:4), which is the devil. The world is where the battle takes place between truth and error, light and darkness. The apostle John sums it up this way:

> Do not love the world or anything in the world. If anyone loves the world, love for the Father is not in them. For everything in the world—the lust of the flesh, the lust of the eyes, and the pride of life—comes not from the Father but from the world. The world and its desires pass away, but whoever does the will of God lives forever. (1 John 2:15–17)

Not all things in culture are evil, corrupt, and bad. The culture has reflections of God's beauty and goodness. However, behind much of the culture war is a spiritual war where the three aspects of warfare—the world, the flesh, and the devil—can conspire together to influence and shape a culture so that it expresses itself in opposition to Christ and His best for humanity. This conspiracy against Christ manifests itself in art, entertainment, politics, sports, education, and business.

The flesh

Spiritual warfare isn't only something that takes place *out there* in the world—it's also in our bodies and minds! For some of us, the most intense spiritual battles are fought within ourselves. We can understand the circumstances that the enemy uses to destroy us. We can accept the truth of how the world lures and tempts us. We can understand, to some degree, that the battle in the spiritual realm is ongoing and real, even though we cannot see it. But getting a grasp on what is going on within our own hearts and minds can be the hardest, most exhausting, battle of all.

It's interesting that the word "compromise" is comprised of two words: "com" and "promise." It literally means to come together to make an agreement with a promise.[1] This is where my internal battle rages strong. Maybe like you, I wrestle with the voices in my own mind that are constantly making the wrong agreements with lies that are opposed to God's promises. The seed of compromise bears the fruits of the flesh: self-doubt, shame, resentment, lust, and envy.

Where these unhealthy agreements fester and linger, they manifest in my flesh in a compromising life of sin.

Paul describes better than anyone the struggle that Christians experience against their flesh: "I know that nothing good dwells in me, that is, in my flesh. For I have the desire to do what is right, but not the ability to carry it out. For I do not do the good I want, but the evil I do not want is what I keep on doing. Now if I do what I do not want, it is no longer I who do it, but sin that dwells within me" (Rom. 7:18–20 ESV).

Yet Paul knows that God has not left us to fight sin on our own. He assures us that "it is God who works in you, both to will and to work for his good pleasure" (Phil. 2:13 ESV). The Spirit of God who works in us is at war with the passions and desires of our flesh, which run contrary to God's will. We overcome the flesh not by sheer determination or self-discipline, but by surrendering to God's power at work within us. The flesh constantly pulls us toward selfish desires, but the Spirit gives us the strength to resist and rise above them. God's power enables us to say "no" to sin and "yes" to holiness, transforming our hearts from the inside out. As we abide in Christ, His Spirit renews our minds, aligns our desires with His, and empowers us to live in victory rather than defeat.

As we partner with God's power and presence, and as we make new agreements with His promises, we walk in His Spirit and our desires are gradually transformed. What once tempted the flesh loses its grip, because the Spirit rewires our hearts and aligns our longings with God's will.

Sin no longer rules when we are rooted in Him. The deeper the roots, the less our flesh craves the wrong desires. Self-effort can attempt to cage the flesh, but only God's Spirit can crucify it.

Paul contrasts the fruit of the Spirit with the works of the flesh in Galatians 5:19–23. These are the manifestations of the flesh: impurity, sensuality, immorality, idolatry, sorcery, drunkenness, carousing, strife, jealousy, outbursts of anger, dissensions, disputes, factions, and things like these. If one looks at the list, it begins with moral sins (impurity, immorality, sensuality); then moves on to religious sins first (idolatry, sorcery); and then concludes with social sins (drunkenness, carousing, strife, jealousy, outbursts of anger, dissensions, disputes, factions).

In contrast, there is a difference with the fruit of the Spirit. The Spirit of Christ produces "love, joy, peace, patience, kindness, goodness, faithfulness, gentleness, self-control" (Gal. 5:22–23 ESV).

We can approach spiritual warfare with victory because of our union with Christ, who secured that victory on the cross. Obsessing over sin is not the way to overcome our sin. Being united with Christ means we stay rooted in Him. His life empowers our desires to align with His. Daily surrender, walking in the Spirit, and fixing our eyes on Him rewires our hearts. Sin may tempt, but it no longer reigns; obedience flows because His life flows through us. We don't fight to obtain victory; we abide, and in abiding, we are already victorious.

Therefore, Paul admonishes, "walk by the Spirit, and you

will not gratify the desires of the flesh" (Gal. 5:16). One cannot overcome the flesh by self-effort or self-resolution, but by submitting to the Holy Spirit. Satan, on the other hand, allies with our flesh, enticing us with the desires of our hearts and planting subtle lies that cause us to doubt the truth about who God is and what He has said about Himself.

The devil

The primary adversary in spiritual warfare is a very real being called Satan, whose name means "adversary." He is also referred to as "the devil," which means slanderer or accuser. Peter warns, "Be alert and of sober mind. Your enemy the devil prowls around like a roaring lion looking for someone to devour" (1 Peter 5:8). Satan's objective is to lead believers away from God through deceit, temptation, and accusation.

For some people, the idea of the devil seems ridiculous. It conjures up images of a cartoon figure with horns and a pitchfork. But the Bible is clear that there is a real opponent of God and of our souls. We know that Satan was created by God, so he's not a rival or equal opposing force to God but rather a prideful rebel who will employ any means necessary to get his way. He's constantly scheming about how he can inflict misery on humankind, and especially about how he can separate God's creation from a loving relationship with its Creator.

SATAN'S OBJECTIVE: STEAL, KILL AND DESTROY. JESUS' OBJECTIVE: GIVE US LIFE TO THE FULL.

As Paul points out, Satan is "the spirit who is now at work in those who are disobedient" (Eph. 2:2), and the world and the flesh come into conflict with God when they follow Satan's lead. Even though Satan isn't omnipotent or omnipresent, he heads the rebellion against God. His character and schemes actively embody every aspect of what is abhorrent in the eyes of a holy, just, and loving God.

In John 10:10 we see the objective of Jesus contrasted with the objective of the devil: "The thief comes only to steal and kill and destroy; I have come that they may have life, and have it to the full." Satan's objective: steal, kill and destroy. Jesus' objective: give us life to the full.

Drilling Down on the Devil

In light of Satan's desire to destroy us, and since he works in and through the world and our flesh, we need to drill down a little further on his tactics in this war.

Satan is stealthy and a schemer

Peter challenges us to be aware of the enemy's tactics and deceptions. The devil "prowls around like a roaring lion" (1 Peter 5:8). I have spent many days hunting in the mountains of the Pacific Northwest, and I always carry a sidearm for defense against our native mountain lions, also known as cougars. They are notorious for being stealthy predators. How much more should we stay alert against the enemy of our souls?

Paul gives us a similar exhortation: "Put on the full armor of God, so that you can take your stand against the devil's schemes" (Eph. 6:11). The Greek word for schemes is *methodeia,* and it carries the idea of cunning arts, deceit, craft, or trickery. That means your enemy's attacks aren't always obvious. So let me ask you: How is your spiritual sobriety? Are you aware of the enemy's schemes to entrap you?

Satan is a thief, a liar, and a murderer

Satan's endgame is to steal God's glory. If he cannot dethrone God in heaven, he will try to dethrone God in hearts. Consider the lie he used to spiral humanity into a world of sin and brokenness in the garden of Eden. Despite God's clear warning to Adam and Even that eating from a particular tree would result in death, Satan said, "You will not certainly die" (Gen. 3:4). He then attacked God's character, telling Eve, "For God knows that when you eat from it your eyes will be opened, and you will be like God, knowing good and evil" (Gen. 3:4–5).

Satan's main goal is to rob God of His worship by doing two things. First, he wants to convince you to worship at the altar of Self. Second, he wants to convince you that God is unworthy of your trust. You will never worship One whom you don't trust. The character of God is on trial, and Satan is the accuser seeking to paint a picture of God as the great villain. He is the ultimate gaslighter. We moved from the lies of secularization (God is not real) to the lies of victimization (God is not good).

Paul warned the Corinthian church so that they wouldn't fall into the same demonic trap that Satan employed in the garden of Eden. He says, "But I am afraid that just as Eve was deceived by the serpent's cunning, your minds may somehow be led astray from your sincere and pure devotion to Christ" (2 Cor. 11:3–4).

We were created to worship the Creator, not creation. This misplaced worship is what also started the diabolic spiral of debauchery and rebellion that Paul warned the Romans about: "Therefore God gave them over in the sinful desires of their hearts to sexual impurity for the degrading of their bodies with one another. They exchanged the truth about God for a lie, and worshiped and served created things rather than the Creator—who is forever praised. Amen" (Rom. 1:24–25).

Jesus called Satan "the father of lies" and a "murderer" (John 8:44). Like a scene out of a detective crime show, the devil commits spiritual homicide, and his weapon of choice is a lie.

Fighting in the Wrong Way

Christians who see that there's a battle to be fought need to be aware of one of Satan's other schemes, namely, to get us to fight in the wrong way. It's startling how spiritually naive many believers are. Satan dupes them into giving their allegiance to him, even as they think they are serving the mission of Jesus.

Consider the moment when Jesus rebukes Peter by stating in Matthew 16:23, "Get behind me, Satan! You are a stumbling block to me; you do not have in mind the concerns of God, but merely human concerns."

"Get behind me, Satan" seems harsh and out of character for Jesus, especially when addressing Peter, one of His most devout disciples. Why did Jesus say this? What was it Peter did to deserve such a rebuke? Without knowing it, Peter was speaking for Satan. Peter was inadvertently being used by Satan in thinking he was protecting Jesus. Although Peter had just moments before declared Jesus as the Christ, he turned from God's perspective and viewed the situation from man's perspective, which brought about a stern rebuke.

We must also see how easily we can become an unwitting spokesperson for Satan. This is especially true when we lose sight of God's plan for us. This comes about when our focus is on our careers, our possessions, our security, and the things of the world rather than on sacrifice and service and the proclaiming of God's message.

Master of Deception

The Bible also describes Satan as a counterfeit who "masquerades as an angel of light" (2 Cor. 11:14). Satan redefines the truth and puts his perverted spin on it. This has become a modern-day Trojan horse. Believers are abandoning God's definition of good and evil or right and wrong and adopting Satan's reclassification. Satan's strategy is simple: make sin look normal and righteousness look strange.[2]

We are living in similar days to when Isaiah called out to Israel, "Woe to those who call evil good and good evil, who put darkness for light and light for darkness, who put bitter for sweet and sweet for bitter" (Isa. 5:20). When society begins defending sins as if they were morally good, and condemning moral goodness as evil, it's a catastrophe. In our digital culture, if you can get it trending, people accept it as true.

Counterfeit Love and the Great Redefinition

Compromise rarely walks through the front door; it slips in disguised as virtue. Today, the enemy doesn't just oppose truth—he rebrands it. Biblical words are still being used—grace, love, justice, and truth—but they've been hollowed out and filled with demonic definitions. This is the age of the counterfeit.

We are watching part of a generation fall away, not because they've rejected Christianity outright, but because they've embraced a version of it that's been edited by culture and baptized in lies. Today, love means affirming everything. And if you don't, you're labeled hateful. But real love doesn't mean affirming a lie; it means telling the truth, even when it hurts.

Jesus loved people enough to call them out of darkness, not coddle them in it. In our culture, love has become god instead of God becoming our love. We worship the feeling of love, the language of love, the appearance of love, but without the truth and holiness of the God who is love. Discernment has never been more vital. The most dangerous deception is the one that uses Bible language with hell's agenda.

So don't chase the counterfeit. Don't trade truth for acceptance. We were never called to blend in; we were called to stand firm. Paul explains this in a letter he wrote to his protégé, Timothy: "Opponents must be gently instructed, in the hope that God will grant them repentance leading them to a knowledge of the truth, and that they will come to their senses and escape from the trap of the devil, who has taken them captive to do his will" (2 Tim. 2:25–26).

Far too many are being held captive to execute and carry out the devil's will. God desires to see them "come to their senses," to awaken from demonic deceptions that have blinded them to Satan's loyalty. Some are held captive and blinded by ignorance: They follow evil thinking that they are helping God. Some are held captive and blinded by arrogance: They follow evil knowing they are fighting God.

The Rape of the Mind by Joost A. M. Meerloo explores how totalitarian regimes, including the Nazis, used psychological tactics to control and break the human spirit. Through "menticide," the calculated destruction of individual thought, Nazi leaders employed fear, propaganda, and repetitive indoctrination to erase personal convictions and replace them with blind obedience. Meerloo warns that by eroding critical thinking and promoting blind conformity, menticide becomes a powerful tool for controlling entire populations.

Maybe we don't use that word in our everyday conversations, but the concept is played out in our everyday lives. This is why Jesus connected the dots between Satan being a liar, or chief propagandist, and a murderer. He was revealing the sinister plot of Satan to use lies and deception to commit spiritual genocide against the human race.

Jesus Shows Us the Way

We see this battle strategy play out in the life of Jesus multiple times. The first time we get a front-row seat to this theater of war is when Jesus faced the devil head-on in the desert after fasting for forty days.

In the first temptation, Satan says to Jesus, "If you are the Son of God, tell these stones to become bread" (Matt. 4:3). The temptation to sin was not in the act of turning stones into bread; we know Jesus turned water into wine (John 2:1–10). So what was the big deal behind this temptation?

Beneath the surface of these words, Satan is attacking the identity of Jesus by trying to plant the seed of doubt about His Sonship, enticing Him to prove His worth through a miracle. Jesus used Scripture to battle Satan's temptation, not some elaborate spiritual power inaccessible to us. Jesus responds by saying, "It is written: 'Man shall not live on bread alone, but on every word that comes from the mouth of God'" (Matt. 4:4).

In this moment, Jesus wielded the truth of the Father's words and refused to take the bait of proving His worth. With one final stab, Jesus penetrated Satan's armor and delivered an almost fatal wound, and Satan fled from the scene!

Jesus didn't just win for you, He showed you how to win. And now, you walk in that same Spirit, not as a passive victim of lies, but as a Spirit-filled warrior, grounded in truth and clothed in power. Spiritual warfare isn't a battle you fight with *your* strength; it's a battle you walk in with Christ. Speak truth, pray boldly, obey faithfully, and watch the enemy crumble before the power of the Spirit. "The reason the Son of God appeared was to destroy the works of the devil" (1 John 3:8 ESV).

Remember, you are no match for the adversity you are facing. But the adversity you are facing is no match for the Spirit you possess.

2

Heart Check: The Choice of Allegiance

The revolution of Jesus is in the first place and continuously a revolution of the human heart.

– DALLAS WILLARD

The room was quiet. Just a circle of NBA players, a deck of cards, and a single poker chip in each hand. During the pregame chapel, I spread the cards slowly across the table: a royal flush, the unbeatable hand. But this wasn't about poker. On each card, I had written something deeper, something eternal. His Presence. His Power. His Purpose. His Perspective. His Provision.

Then I held up the chip.

In poker, when you believe in your hand, and when you're confident it's unbeatable, you push all your chips in. No hesitation. No backup plan. You go all in.

I looked around the room. "That's what God is inviting you into. Not a half-hearted faith. Not a Sunday-only spirituality. He's not asking for a slice of your life; He's asking for all of it. And when you know who He is, when you've seen His power, felt His presence, and trusted His provision, you realize it's not a gamble. It's a guarantee."

One by one, they picked up their chips and wrote the words "ALL IN."

Late in the third quarter, I noticed one of our players who had been in chapel that night running away from the bench to the tunnel that led to the locker room. I didn't think much of it until I saw his teammate, who was also in chapel that night, run after him down the tunnel. I could sense something was off, and the Holy Spirit prompted me to make my way to the locker room and check on my brothers.

As I walked into the locker room, both men were sitting on a weight bench facing each other. These were not simply players on a professional basketball team. These were my brothers in Christ, and we had developed a bond that season. As I walked closer to check in, I realized that one of the guys was in tears with his head down. We have all hit those moments of breakdown, and as men, we are told we can't express our emotions and vulnerabilities. When I asked how my brother was doing, he slowly raised his head with tears in his face and boldly said two words:

"All IN."

In this moment, his "all in" was not just lip service. It was a surrender of his heart to trust Jesus as the source of His comfort and strength in the midst of pressure and pain.

In a culture built on compromise, half-truths, and halfway commitments, a fully surrendered heart is radical. It's compelling. It stands out. Because when the world hedges its bets, God calls us to push everything to the center and trust that His hand never loses.

The War for the Heart

We often think the culture war is about headlines, elections, or hashtags. But the real battlefield isn't in Washington or Hollywood. It's the human heart. The culture war is just the symptom. The heart war is the source.

In every generation, a war rages that few can see but all can feel. It's not just political or social. It's deeper than ideology or philosophy. It is a war for the heart: a war between two counterfeit ways of living that both resist the kingdom of God. One is loud and defiant; the other quiet and self-assured. One screams for independence; the other hides behind tradition. But both are equally dangerous.

This is the spiritual clash between what I'm calling the rebellious spirit and the religious spirit.

The rebellious spirit: "I will not bow"

The rebellious spirit thrives in a culture that exalts self as the ultimate authority. In our day, it wears many faces:

radical individualism, sexual autonomy, the rejection of absolute truth, and the deconstruction of historic Christian faith.

The rebellious spirit doesn't merely say, "God doesn't exist." It says, "Even if He does, I choose me." This spirit can be traced back to the Garden of Eden. Despite the fact that God had given clear commands, the serpent whispered to Eve, "Did God really say . . . ?" (Gen. 3:1).That same voice whispers still, "You can be your own god. Define good and evil for yourself."

The apostle Paul describes the rebellious spirit vividly: "They exchanged the truth about God for a lie, and worshiped and served created things rather than the Creator" (Rom. 1:25).

It's not hard to see this spirit at work in today's culture. We see it on our screens, in our schools, and in our politics; it is redefining identity and reshaping morality. But it's not just out *there*; it lives in every heart that resists God's authority.

The rebellious spirit declares war on God's reign. It breaks commandments with pride and calls it freedom. It demands tolerance but has no room for repentance. And, tragically, it promises liberty while delivering chains.

The religious spirit: "I will appease God"

In contrast to the rebellious spirit, the religious spirit appears noble, even moral. It prizes order, tradition, and outward obedience. But at its core, it's driven not by love for God but by a desire to earn His approval and control others.

The religious spirit doesn't seek to *please* God but rather to *appease* God.

This is the spirit of the older brother in the story of the prodigal son (Luke 15:11–32). He never left home. He did everything "right." Yet when the father lavished grace on his younger brother, the brother who left home and rebelled but later returned in repentance, the religious son became angry. Why? Because he believed blessing must be earned, not given.

The religious spirit whispers that life must be polished, curated, and perfect, a life of performance that earns man's applause but doesn't rest in God's approval. It blinds the eyes to grace, binds the heart with rules, and turns devotion into duty. The religious spirit seeks to appease God instead of truly pleasing Him.

The Pharisees in Jesus' day embodied this spirit. They tithed meticulously, fasted publicly, and obeyed outwardly, but their hearts were far from God. Jesus said, "These people honor me with their lips, but their hearts are far from me" (Matt. 15:8). Jesus connected the dots between their religious performance and the spirit motivating them when He declared, "You belong to your father, the devil" (John 8:44).

The apostle Paul uncovered a religious spirit driving the Galatian church, a church that was being seduced and influenced by those who promoted living under the law rather than living by faith based on the abundant life provided by the renewing work of the Holy Spirit (Gal. 3:1–6). Likewise, Paul warned Timothy of those who follow "deceitful spirits and things taught by demons" and thus lead people away from simple faith in Christ into lifeless rules and asceticism (1 Tim. 4:1). This is the essence of the religious spirit: It substitutes man-made regulations and performance for intimacy with God. What looks like holiness on the surface is actually demonic deception, because it shifts trust from the finished work of Christ to self-effort and control.

The religious spirit is like living in a continuous spiritual audit. Audits can work great for a business but not for abiding in Christ. Like an overzealous accountant, the religious spirit seeks to meticulously balance the ledger while measuring every failure and misstep, not just in yourself but in everyone around you. It's about performance over presence; grades over grace; comparison over compassion.

In responding to a culture characterized by rebellion, it's all too easy for Christians to fall prey to a religious spirit. This kind of spirit builds walls instead of bridges. It confuses religiosity with transformation. And like the rebellious spirit, it resists the lordship of Christ, but it does so from a pew instead of a protest.

Though they look like opposites, the rebellious spirit and religious spirit are deeply connected. They are both ways to live independently from God. The rebel spirit says, "I don't need God. I'll be my own master." The religious spirit says, "I'll be so good that I don't need God's mercy."

Both are rooted in pride, and both miss the heart of the gospel.

The Gospel: A Third Way

Jesus didn't come to make bad people good (as the religious spirit believes), nor did He come to give people permission to be their own gods (as the rebellious spirit claims). He came to make dead people alive, to restore broken people into a relationship with the Father.

The way of Jesus is neither rebellion nor religion. It is redemption. In Christ, we are set free from sin (rebellion) by His blood and set free from striving (religion) by His grace. We have been called into a relationship where our identity is not earned or self-made but received. The gospel confronts the rebel with truth: "You are not the center of the universe." The gospel confronts the religious with grace: "You can't earn what God freely gives."

Jesus modeled both grace and truth (John 1:14). He ate with sinners and rebuked Pharisees. He exposed sin but extended mercy. He offered identity, not based on performance, but on the love of the Father.

So how does all this affect the way we respond to the culture? We do not bow to culture, but neither do we condemn it from a distance. We speak the truth boldly, but with tears in our eyes. We walk in holiness, not to prove our worth, but because we already belong. We offer a third way, the way of Jesus: crucified pride, surrendered hearts, and redeemed lives.

The church engages culture by doing more than issuing statements or joining debates. True influence comes when we combine a firm stand on biblical truth with tangible acts of love and service. We take a stand on issues like life, justice, and sexuality, while also walking alongside people in their struggles, feeding the hungry, supporting the vulnerable, mentoring the lost, and listening with grace. This kind of engagement communicates that our convictions are rooted not in judgment but in the heart of God, showing that truth and compassion are inseparable. In this way, the church bears witness to both the authority of God's Word and the radical love of Christ.

Managing Hearts vs. Redeeming Hearts

Living out this third way, the "gospel way," does not mean that a society doesn't need laws. In any just society, laws are essential. They provide structure, define right and wrong, protect the vulnerable, and promote the common good. But civil laws have limits. They can expose sin. They can restrain evil. They can prescribe consequences. But they cannot redeem the human heart, because external rules can never produce internal transformation.

This is true for God's law as well. Biblical commands may keep people from sinning outwardly due to fear of punishment, but they don't remove the desire to sin. Someone might not steal because stealing is illegal, yet still be consumed with envy and greed. They might not commit adultery because of reputational consequences, yet still be unfaithful in their heart. Paul says that "no one will be declared righteous in God's sight by the works of the law; rather, through the law we become conscious of our sin" (Rom. 3:20).

The law reveals how far we've fallen, but it doesn't lift us up. That's the job of grace.

For Christians, advocating for laws that reflect God's values, like protecting life, promoting justice, honoring marriage, and defending human dignity is not just cultural engagement; it's part of our call to be salt and light (Matt. 5:13–16).

But laws, no matter how righteous, have limits. The apostle Paul made this abundantly clear, saying, "Now we know that the law is good, if one uses it properly. We also know that the law is made not for the righteous but for lawbreakers" (1 Tim. 1:8–9).

EXTERNAL RULES CAN NEVER PRODUCE INTERNAL TRANSFORMATION.

The law can expose sin. It can restrain evil. It can prescribe consequences. But it cannot redeem the human heart. Why? Because external rules can never produce internal transformation.

Only Christ Can Transform the Heart

A few years ago I was in the backwoods bow-hunting bull elk. As the herd was moving up the steep ridge, I decided to make the chase and attempt to get ahead of them to set up a shot. In the process, I suffered an episode of AFib, which means my heart was beating over 160 beats a minute and couldn't slow down. It felt like a heart attack, and I ended up being flown to the ER. The good news was that it was treatable, and a procedure called an ablation reset my irregular heartbeat and put it back into rhythm. After the procedure, the difference was like night and day; it was like getting a superpower of strength and endurance.

How many of us are suffering from a heart condition that is throwing us out of rhythm with God and others? God is our heavenly cardiologist. He knows the deepest chambers of our hearts, understands every beat, and diagnoses what threatens our spiritual life. He repairs what is broken, clears blockages of sin and fear, and strengthens what is weak so that our hearts can pump life, love, and faith throughout our lives.

Jesus did what the law could never do. He didn't come just to reform society; He came to redeem sinners. This requires a new heart, which is what God promised to His people long ago: "I will give you a new heart and put a new spirit in you" (Ezek. 36:26).

The gospel is about heart surgery, not just behavior modification. It reaches into the deepest parts of our soul, rooting out sin, shame, and self-worship and replacing it with a new identity, a new power, and a new desire to love and obey God, not out of duty but out of delight.

When someone is transformed by Christ, they don't just obey the law externally; they are changed from the inside out. This is what makes Christianity radically different from moralism. Moralism demands righteousness without giving the power to achieve it. Grace empowers us to live holy lives because we've been made new.

In light of Jesus' transforming work, the church has a prophetic role in relation to the culture. We hold up the law as a mirror that reveals people's need for a Savior, but we must never stop there. If all we offer is moral outrage and not gospel hope, we become harsh judges rather than humble ambassadors of reconciliation.

So yes, we fight for laws that reflect God's justice, but we fight harder to bring people to the cross, where law meets love and judgment meets mercy. People don't just need better laws. They need new hearts.

Examining Our Own Hearts

The word "heart" appears over seven hundred times in the Bible, making it one of the most common anthropological terms in Scripture. Our hearts are designed to love God wholly, and yet our hearts desire many things besides God.

The condition of your heart determines the health of your relationship with God and with others. Jesus said, "For it is from within, out of a person's heart, that evil thoughts come—sexual immorality, theft, murder, adultery, greed, malice, deceit, lewdness, envy, slander, arrogance and folly. All these evils come from inside and defile a person" (Mark 7:21–23).

How sobering! Jesus addresses not only our behavior but also our attitude, and even our secret sins. So much of our lives are focused on what's above the surface, but Jesus is after what lies beneath the surface: the heart. In light of the crucial role the heart plays in our spiritual life, here are some steps to make sure it's functioning properly.

Guard your heart

"Above all else, guard your heart, for everything you do flows from it" (Prov. 4:23). Guarding your heart means to be careful about what you welcome into your life. It means being wise and filtering what you look at, listen to, and allow to influence you. It calls for humility, confession and repentance, and being honest with God about the things that tempt you. The longer you linger in sin and temptation, the more your heart will be poisoned by them.

Align your heart

"Love the LORD your God with all your heart and with all your soul and with all your strength" (Deut. 6:5 NIV). Aligning your heart with God mean to set your affections on Him and desire Him more than anything. It means to live in response to what He desires for you, admitting and confessing that you have idols like greed, comfort, entitlement, and selfishness. When your heart is aligned with His, it values what He values.

Pour out your heart

"He heals the brokenhearted and binds up their wounds" (Ps. 147:3). Receiving healing for your heart starts with honesty before God. You bring to Him all of your hurts, regrets, disappointments, and fears, acknowledging that He is your only hope for transformation. This is a process of daily dependence upon the Holy Spirit to restore what was broken while taking steps to cooperate with Him in His healing work (granting forgiveness, seeking restoration, praying for our enemies, etc.). God alone has the power to take your brokenness and bring beauty.

Blessings of a Pure Heart

As we learn to pursue a healthy heart, removing what harms and nurturing what heals, we position ourselves to receive the blessings that flow from a pure heart. Health prepares the soil; purity produces the fruit. Jesus said, “Blessed are the pure in heart, for they will see God” (Matt. 5:8).

Biblical purity isn’t only about moral behavior or avoiding obvious sins. It’s about having a singular focus, a heart undivided in its love for God. A pure heart is one that wants God more than anything else. It’s wholehearted, not half-hearted. And that kind of heart shines in a darkened age. Consider how a pure heart positions us to receive and perceive blessings from God.

A pure heart exposes pretending

We live in a world full of filters, literal and metaphorical. People project curated versions of themselves to gain approval, build a platform, or chase acceptance. But when someone walks with a pure heart—humble, honest, and God-focused—it pierces through the fog of pretense. There’s no hidden agenda, no manipulation, no moral duplicity. Just simple, sincere faith. That kind of integrity isn’t just admirable; it’s magnetic. It exposes the shallow, and invites others to long for something deeper and truer.

A pure heart builds trust

A pure-hearted person is safe. They don’t gossip, flatter, or scheme. Their motives are clean. You can sense when someone is driven by genuine love rather than self-interest. In a world where manipulation and betrayal are common, someone with a pure heart becomes a refuge of trust. That's why Paul told Timothy: "The goal of this command is love, which comes from a pure heart" (1 Tim. 1:5). When love flows from a pure heart, it's not performative or transactional. It's deeply trustworthy, and people are drawn to it.

A pure heart radiates joy and peace

The pure in heart aren't anxious to be someone they're not. They're not caught in comparison, shame, or deceit. They walk in the light, and with that comes freedom. Their joy isn't based on applause or achievements, it's rooted in intimacy with God. That kind of joy is rare in a distracted, anxious culture. It's not loud, but it's radiant. And people will start asking, "Where does that peace come from?"

A pure heart sees God

Jesus' promise is astonishing: The pure in heart will "see God" (Matt. 5:8). Purity sharpens our spiritual vision. It gives us the ability to see God at work in pain, in beauty, in people, in purpose. And when others see someone whose life is deeply aligned with God, it awakens spiritual hunger. Purity isn't just private; it becomes prophetic. It points beyond itself to a better kingdom and a better King.

But as we pursue a pure heart, it's important to remember that a pure heart (on this side of heaven) doesn't mean a flawless heart.

Purity Isn't Perfection—It's Pursuit

A pure heart is a focused heart, a heart that returns again and again to the feet of Jesus, repenting, surrendering, and seeking. That kind of vulnerability is compelling too. It says to the world, "I'm not perfect, but I'm not pretending. I need Jesus."

That kind of honesty is rare and beautiful. The culture may mock, but it's watching. Our world may celebrate rebellion, self-expression, and moral "freedom," but underneath the noise, there is a deep hunger for wholeness, truth, and hope. A pure heart stands out. Not because it shouts the loudest, but because it shines the brightest.

> **OUR WORLD MAY CELEBRATE REBELLION, SELF-EXPRESSION, AND MORAL "FREEDOM," BUT UNDERNEATH THE NOISE, THERE IS A DEEP HUNGER FOR WHOLENESS, TRUTH, AND HOPE.**

And in the end, the person with a pure heart will not only see God more clearly but they will also help others see Him too.

3

Consecration: Purging the Idols from Our Lives

Man's nature, so to speak, is a perpetual factory of idols.

– JOHN CALVIN

It started with a fire. Not the kind that burns buildings, but the kind that burns idols.

In Acts 19, the city of Ephesus, a place drenched in magic, idolatry, and wealth, erupted in revival. The apostle Paul had been preaching there for two years, and the Spirit of God was cutting deep. People weren't just agreeing with his message; they were being undone by it. And then something radical happened: "A number who had practiced sorcery brought their scrolls together and and burned them publicly" (Acts 19:19).

EPHESUS TEACHES US SOMETHING THE MODERN CHURCH OFTEN FORGETS: YOU CAN'T HAVE REVIVAL WITHOUT REPENTANCE.

These weren't storybooks. These were sacred tools of power, reputation, and identity. Their value was staggering: 50,000 silver pieces, the equivalent of millions today. And they didn't sell them. They didn't donate them. They burned them. Because when your heart is pierced by the holiness of God, you don't manage idols. You destroy them.

It wasn't just a fire. It was a funeral, for who they used to be.

This scene in Ephesus teaches us something the modern church often forgets: You can't have revival without repentance. You can't have consecration without confrontation. The idols in our lives, like success, comfort, image, control, and relationships, don't leave politely. They must be surrendered, dragged into the light, and consumed. A compelling faith is a burning faith.

That fire in Ephesus wasn't about rage; it was about release. It wasn't about shame; it was about freedom. This is consecration: the courageous, often costly, act of letting go of the things that grip your heart more than God does. This kind of idol purging is critical not only for our own personal holiness but also for our witness.

Hypocrisy Undermines Our Credibility

In an age where charisma often overshadows character, we need to recover a sobering reality: You can't have a prophetic voice with a profane lifestyle. Being prophetic is not merely about foretelling the future or having a platform to speak from; it's about bearing God's heart, embodying His holiness, and calling people back to His truth. And God does not entrust His weighty words to those who treat His presence lightly.

When most of us hear the word "profanity," we instantly think about words we shouldn't speak rather than lives we shouldn't live. But to live a profane lifestyle means to take what is sacred and treat it as ordinary. It's when the holy is handled casually. It's when compromise becomes normalized, sin is excused, and the fear of God is replaced by the approval of man. Being prophetic isn't about popularity; it's about consecration. God raises up those who have been with Him in the secret place, not those chasing relevance in public spaces.

When our lifestyle contradicts our message, our voice loses credibility. People may still listen to our content, but they'll no longer trust our character. The world is not looking for another viral Christian; it's longing for a visible Christ. Jesus had harsh words for those who honored God with their lips but whose hearts were far from Him (Matt. 15:8). A false prophet is dangerous and reckless, and so is a true one who becomes polluted.

If we want to speak with fire, we must be refined by it.

Take, for example, John the Baptist. He didn't just preach repentance; he lived in the wilderness, clothed in humility, and he burned with holy zeal. He didn't chase crowds. The crowds came to him because his voice carried weight. Why? Because he had been set apart by God; his life matched his message. A prophetic voice is not earned through giftedness. It is verified through holiness.

IF WE WANT TO SPEAK WITH FIRE, WE MUST BE REFINED BY IT.

You cannot call people to the altar while dancing around idols. You cannot confront darkness if you're still making peace with it. You cannot pierce hearts if your own is numb with compromise. If we proclaim the words of God, we must be marked by the character of God. As the psalmist put it, "The LORD confides in those who fear Him; He makes His covenant known to them" (Ps. 25:14).

Identifying Idols

So if we want to purge the idols from our lives, we need to know what an idol is and how we can recognize it in our lives today. An idol is anything we value above God, anything that takes the place of God in our hearts and draws our attention away from Him.

Maybe we are drawn to certain relationships that God has repeatedly warned us to quit. Perhaps it's the pursuit of status, fame, or wealth. Many have made idols out of political figures and celebrities, investing more energy and time into thinking about them than they do communing with the very God who created them. Likewise, people idolize ideas and ideologies. They hold onto a political belief system with greater conviction than the Word of God. People also make idols of things like social media, fashion, children, careers, expensive cars, or even (Lord, help me) their phones.

Not everything listed above is inherently sinful. However, when we embrace anything in an unhealthy way and derive our primary sense of worth and identity from it, we're guilty of idolatry. The only response to idols is to purge them from our lives. And when we do, we'll find on the other side of that purge is freedom.

The Hidden Altars

We don't bow to golden calves anymore. But we bow. Every day. We bow to our screens. We bow to applause. We bow to our carefully manicured image, our cravings for control, and our addiction to comfort.

We may not explicitly deny God with our mouth, but we deny Him with our lifestyle. We sing songs on Sunday while secretly sacrificing our hearts at altars of self, success, and significance. We are idolaters in disguise. We claim Jesus is Lord, but we follow the commands of culture. We say we trust God, yet we panic when our bank account dips, our influence shrinks, or our prayers go unanswered.

We scroll for hours but pray for minutes. We compare endlessly, consume thoughtlessly, and wonder why we feel so anxious, empty, and spiritually numb. The problem isn't that God has changed. The problem is that we've replaced Him.

We have elevated good things into god things, and they are failing us. Let's examine some of the most popular idols of our time.

Idol #1: The self

We live in the age of self-worship where the gospel of "follow your heart" has replaced "take up your cross." The truest modern god is me: *my* truth, *my* brand, *my* dreams. We don't just love ourselves; we worship ourselves. But the self was never meant to be a god. It was meant to die daily so Christ can live through us.

Idol #2: Comfort

We pray for God to move, as long as it doesn't disrupt our plans. We want a safe Jesus—a Jesus who blesses but never demands obedience. We forget that the cross is not a metaphor for mild inconvenience; it's a call to die. We don't suffer well because we've been discipled to believe that following Jesus should make life easier.

Idol #3: Approval

We've traded the approval of God for the applause of people. We edit our beliefs to be palatable. We water down truth to avoid offense. We forget that Jesus said, "Woe to you when everyone speaks well of you" (Luke 6:26). You cannot carry your cross and your reputation at the same time.

Idol #4: Control

We crave predictability more than we crave the presence of God. When life slips from our grip, we question God's goodness instead of surrendering to it. But faith is never about control. It is always about surrender. Sometimes God lets your plans fall apart so that your idols will too.

Idol #5: Religion

Yes, even religion can be an idol. We can be so obsessed with the appearance of godliness that we stop pursuing God Himself. We polish our morality, perfect our theology, and miss the one thing Jesus truly wants—our hearts.

Idol #6: Pleasure

Pleasure is the quiet god of our age, demanding nothing but our undivided devotion to feeling good. We binge, scroll, consume, and indulge, numbing our souls with counterfeit comforts while calling it "self-care." The altar of pleasure promises life but delivers apathy, addiction, and spiritual dullness. It's not that we don't worship; rather, we worship whatever thrills us most. And in the process, we trade the presence of God for the anesthesia of amusement.

Regardless of which idols we're drawn to, we cannot toy with them. Because idols don't just distract; they devour. They consume our peace, steal our joy, and rob God of the worship He alone deserves. And they will never stop demanding more. More time. More affection. More of you. Until you are numb. Or burned out. Or empty, wondering why the Christian life feels powerless. When it comes to idols, we don't just need more information. We need holy defibrillation. We need to tear down the altars in our hearts and rebuild the throne for Christ alone.

Purging Through Consecration

Purging the idols in our lives involves putting away certain objects, behaviors, habits, and desires. But fleeing idolatry isn't only negative. It also involves worshiping the true God and being consecrated to Him. We should daily dethrone everything that competes with Christ and say with trembling joy, "LORD, you alone are my portion and my cup" (Ps. 16:5). Our hearts should cry out, "Whom have I in heaven but You? And earth has nothing I desire besides You" (Ps. 73:25).

It's time to smash the idols, not manage them. Because until Jesus is enough for you, everything else will try to be. To purge idols and live a consecrated life means to remove anything from our hearts, habits, or priorities that competes with our loyalty to Jesus; it means to set ourselves apart wholly for God's purposes. It is both a rejection of counterfeit gods and a devoted surrender to the one true God.

So what does it mean to consecrate ourselves to God? To be consecrated means to be holy, sacred, reserved for divine use. Not just morally clean, but fully available and deeply devoted. In Scripture, when someone or something was consecrated, it was set apart from common use and dedicated exclusively to God (Ex. 29:1; Rom. 12:1).

To live a consecrated life means saying, "God, you get all of me." No compartments. No negotiations. It means living in such a way that your time, body, desires, and decisions are aligned with His will and purpose revealed in His Word. Pursuing purity, not out of duty, but out of delight in being near Him. This isn't just a suggestion or good advice: this is a declaration and mandate we see all throughout Scripture. For instance, 1 Peter 1:15 says, "But just as He who called you is holy, so be holy in all you do." And Paul instructs Christians to "present your bodies as a living sacrifice, holy and acceptable to God" (Rom. 12:1 ESV).

Why This Matters in Our Culture

In a world chasing self-glory, self-gratification, and self-definition, a consecrated life is radically countercultural. It speaks loudly without shouting.

A consecrated believer lives with conviction in a culture of compromise. They love with purity in a world of confusion. They stand with courage when others bow to fear or popularity. The most powerful witness is not a trendy Christian, but a holy one.

I'm reminded of my friend Iftikar from Pakistan, a man whose faith refuses to be hidden. In a culture where proclaiming Jesus can bring danger, he spoke openly about his commitment to Christ with a courage that was almost tangible. During his visit, he told me, with both reverence and fire, that being persecuted for Jesus was a profound honor.

After a staff meeting, we went to lunch at a nearby restaurant. The chatter of other diners faded as he began to describe the abuse he had endured; the threats, the beatings, the constant pressure to renounce his faith. Then he shared the story that made my heart catch: He had been shot with an AK-47. Without hesitation, he stood in the middle of the restaurant and lifted his shirt, revealing scars that traced across his chest and torso like a map of suffering and survival. His family had received repeated death threats, yet every line on his body, every story of danger, testified to his unwavering conviction to live wholly for the Lord.

I left that lunch humbled, my own struggles feeling small in comparison. Yet his story also planted a seed of courage. It reminds me of the high school boys I know who, in a quiet but powerful act of faith, chose to kneel in prayer on their football field. Their boldness is contagious; their willingness to stand, even in small ways, is an echo of the fearless devotion I saw in Iftikar. Faith, whether in the face of a gun or on a local football field, still has the power to transform hearts and inspire others to live boldly.

You were not made to blend in. You were made to burn: to be set apart, Spirit-filled, and fully alive in Christ. To purge idols and live a consecrated life is not about becoming more religious. It's about becoming fully His. Let the words of Joshua 3:5 build your curiosity and wonder about what God can do with a consecrated life: "Consecrate yourselves, for tomorrow the LORD will do amazing things among you."

4

Beyond Consumption: Feasting on the Goodness of God

O God, I have tasted Thy goodness, and it has both satisfied me and made me thirsty for more.

— **A. W. TOZER**

I didn't plan on having a spiritual moment in an In-N-Out Burger drive-thru. But there I was, window down, soaking in the smell of grilled onions and salty fries, stomach already rejoicing at the thought of that perfect, juicy, simple, legendary "Double-Double." If you know, you know.

I have always been a burger guy. Not fancy ones with brioche buns and aioli, but the kind that make you stop mid-bite and say, "This is it."

But on this particular day, as I sat in the parking lot, unwrapping that perfect stack of beef and cheese like it was a Christmas gift, something strange happened. I had just devoured the last bite. Fries were gone. Cup was dry. And I still wasn't satisfied.

Physically, I was full. But something deeper in me still felt restless. And right there, it hit me: *You've been treating your soul the same way you treat fast food: grab, consume, repeat.*

I was consuming sermons, books, podcasts—spiritual "calories" from every source. But none of it was transforming me. I was full, but not nourished. I had been living in a spiritual version of fast-food consumption. That burger became a mirror.

It was good, but temporary. Tasty, but fleeting. Filling, but not sustaining.

A Culture of Consumption

There's a difference between snacking on God and feasting on Him. In a culture of convenience, we've learned how to consume spirituality the same way we consume food, that is, quick, easy, and on our terms. But the goodness of God isn't meant to be eaten in a drive-thru. It's meant to be dined on. Savored. Feasted upon.

Jesus didn't say, "Come and sample." He said, "I am the bread of life" (John 6:35). He invites us not to taste test, but to sit down and be satisfied.

Many Christians are drowning in content and starving for Christ. We binge on spiritual snacks but rarely slow down for a sacred meal. This chapter is a call back to true intimacy. Back to the slow, rich, satisfying presence of God. Because you don't fight spiritual emptiness with more noise; you fight it by learning to feast on His goodness.

MANY CHRISTIANS ARE DROWNING IN CONTENT AND STARVING FOR CHRIST. WE BINGE ON SPIRITUAL SNACKS BUT RARELY SLOW DOWN FOR A SACRED MEAL.

We live in a culture defined by consumption. We're the sum total of the brands we wear, the possessions we accumulate, the things we own. But consumption is all about self-gratification, and it's antithetical to the calling of God on our lives.

Something beautiful happens when we move from consuming things to craving God. Through prayer, worship, communion with others, and mediation on His Word, the deepest cravings of our soul can be satisfied. We begin to refuse the toxic junk food of the world in order to feast on the goodness of God.

The Table of Delight vs. the Buffet of Demand

In a culture driven by convenience, customization, and consumerism, Christianity is often packaged the same way, offered as a product rather than a Person. Churches compete for attention, believers shop for spiritual experiences, and discipleship gets reduced to downloads, highlights, and likes. In this environment, the call to abide in Christ stands as a stark and holy contrast.

Jesus didn't invite His followers to consume Him as just a means to an end; He invited them to remain, or abide, in Him. The idea of abiding brings us to one of Jesus' most vivid and powerful illustrations of the believer's relationship with Him: the vine and the branches. He says to His disciples, "Abide in me, and I in you. As the branch cannot bear fruit by itself, unless it abides in the vine, neither can you, unless you abide in me" (John 15:4 ESV).

Just as branches can only bear fruit if they abide in the vine, so believers can only glorify the Father through fruitful lives by abiding in Jesus. Jesus was preparing His disciples for His imminent death and departure by instructing them about their calling and mission. He wanted them to see their absolute dependence on Him, so He tells them to abide in Him.

The Christian faith is about union and communion with Jesus. Union with Christ without communion with Christ is joyless Christianity. As Jesus says in verse 5, "I am the vine; you are the branches. Whoever abides in me and I in him, he it is that bears much fruit, for apart from me you can do nothing" (John 15:5 ESV).

Christianity is about far more than holding the right beliefs or adopting the right behaviors. At salvation, we enter into a union with God that changes our legal status. We have the right standing with God now. We also have communion with God. We have access to a life-giving, soul-thrilling, joy-producing communion with God through Christ.

For many Christians, the three words "abide in Me" make a great wall plaque, but if you delve beneath these comforting words, there is little understanding.

The Beauty of Abiding

The word "abide" (*meno* in the Greek) carries the idea of remaining or continuing,[1] which in this case has to do with a relationship with Jesus. To abide in Jesus means to live with a continual connection to Him, drawing life, strength, wisdom, and purpose from Him.

In a world that is over-connected yet lonely, frantically busy yet accomplishing little of eternal value, super-informed but deeply ignorant on what really matters, abiding involves giving Jesus the best of our time. Abiding is relational; consuming is transactional.

When we initially put our faith in Jesus, God declares us righteous (what the Bible calls being "justified") by His grace. This is a once-for-all declaration, and it is made possible because we are united to Christ by faith. But this *union* with Christ that happens at conversion should lead to continual *communion* with Him throughout our lives. Abiding in Christ involves continually communing with Him.

Abiding in a relationship with Jesus is the opposite of consumer Christianity, which treats Jesus like a service provider. Abiding requires presence, patience, and personal engagement. It says, "I want Jesus more than blessings, more than answers, more than benefits." Abiding is about union, not utility.

To help us understand the difference between abiding and consuming, consider this contrast: consuming produces fatigue, while abiding produces fruit.

Jesus promises that when we abide, we will bear much fruit, fruit that lasts (John 15:5, 16). This fruit includes love, joy, peace, character transformation, and the power to impact others.

But consumer Christianity often leads to spiritual fatigue. Consuming content is not the same as cultivating intimacy. You can binge sermons, follow influencers, and attend multiple worship services, and yet still feel empty if you're not rooted in Christ. True fruit doesn't grow from consumption. It grows from communion.

Consuming reinforces self; abiding shapes identity

Abiding in Christ redefines who we are. We are no longer defined by achievements, opinions, or appearances, but by our union with the One who calls us "friend" (John 15:15). We learn to live based on God's love for us, not our performance.

But consumer Christianity often reinforces a self-centered version of faith: "How does this help me? Feed me? Inspire me?" It treats God as a means to a better version of me, rather than the goal being Christ formed in me (Gal. 4:19).

Consuming is comfortable; abiding is costly

Abiding requires pruning. Jesus says, "Every branch that does bear fruit he prunes, that it may bear more fruit" (John 15:2 ESV). Pruning may involve surrender, waiting, repentance, and even pain. It may not always feel good, but its fruit is deep and eternal.

Consumer Christianity avoids discomfort. It says, "Give me the blessings, but not the cross. Give me peace, but don't confront my pride." It's faith without depth, grace without change.

But only through abiding do we learn what it truly means to follow Jesus, not as an idea, but as a way of life. Consumer Christianity leaves people endlessly searching, always looking for the next big thing, the next spiritual thrill, or the next perfect church. And that endless pursuit only deepens our hunger, because it is disconnected from the Source.

ABIDING IN CHRIST REDEFINES WHO WE ARE. WE ARE NO LONGER DEFINED BY ACHIEVEMENTS, OPINIONS, OR APPEARANCES, BUT BY OUR UNION WITH THE ONE WHO CALLS US "FRIEND" (JOHN 15:15).

The Blessings of Abiding

The call to abide in the vine is ultimately a call to stay connected to Jesus, the One in whom true life is found. When you abide in Christ, when your life is rooted in His presence, Word, and love, you begin to live from a Source greater than yourself. You're no longer white-knuckling your way through sin or striving to perform. You're connected to the Vine, and that connection produces fruit, including power, peace, and joy.

Not fake, religious joy, but deep, soul-level delight that comes from knowing you're loved, chosen, and secure in

Christ. As Jesus said, "I have told you this so that my joy may be in you and that your joy may be complete" (John 15:11).

Abiding is like your phone resting in its wireless charging dock. It doesn't strain or hustle to produce power; it simply has to stay connected and aligned, and the energy flows into it. The moment it's pulled away, the battery starts draining again. But when it rests in place, it's constantly renewed, always ready for what's next.

Abiding doesn't just help you fight sin; it makes you free. Consider some of the blessings of abiding.

Abiding starves the flesh and feeds the Spirit

When you abide in Jesus, daily drawing near through prayer, the Word, and surrender, you're not just avoiding sin, you're replacing it with something better. Sin loses its grip when Christ becomes your source of satisfaction. You begin to crave purity over porn, peace over rage, presence over escape.

Abiding roots your identity in love, not shame

Addictions and anger often grow from wounds, insecurity, and deep shame. But Jesus says, "As the Father has loved me, so I have loved you. Abide in my love" (John 15:9). Abiding reminds you who you are, deeply loved, fully known, and never alone. This isn't merely behavior modification; it's soul transformation.

Abiding brings power, not just willpower

Jesus said, "Apart from me you can do nothing" (John 15:5). Willpower might help for a while, but abiding taps into His Spirit-powered strength. You're not fighting your battles alone; you're drawing from His victory, His purity, His peace.

Abiding exposes the lies behind sin

Porn lies to you. Addiction lies to you. Anger lies to you. But as you abide, the light of Christ reveals truth. You begin to discern the counterfeit and choose the real. Freedom doesn't just come from resisting sin, it comes from seeing Jesus as more beautiful.

Abiding transforms your desires

Jesus doesn't just clean up your behavior; He rewires your appetites. Abiding is how your heart begins to want what He wants. You don't just try harder; you love deeper. That's where freedom lives.

Abiding in Christ is not a technique. It's a relationship. And in that relationship, sin's power breaks, your soul heals, and you become someone new from the inside out.

The Compelling Witness of Abiding

Abiding believers live by a different rhythm, a rhythm shaped by eternity, not just the moment. Their convictions, choices, and attitudes come from being connected to Jesus, not culture. They aren't shaped by the news cycle, political trends, or digital algorithms, they are shaped by the Word and presence of God. That difference becomes evident. And that difference is what makes them magnetic.

An abiding Christian, someone who consistently remains rooted in Christ, is profoundly compelling in our culture because they embody what the world desperately wants but cannot manufacture: peace, identity, integrity, purpose, and unshakable love.

An abiding Christian is compelling in today's culture precisely because they contrast so clearly with what the world often offers: noise, distraction, identity confusion, burnout, and surface-level connection. Abiding in Christ means remaining consistently connected to His presence, truth, and love. In doing so, a believer becomes someone whose life radiates substance over image, peace over panic, and purpose over performance.

An abiding Christian doesn't have to shout to be heard. They don't need a platform to be persuasive. Their presence preaches. In a world that is rootless and restless, they are rooted and restful. And because of that, they draw people—not to themselves, but to Christ.

They are compelling because they carry the evidence of a life deeply connected to Jesus.

5

Increasing Capacity: The Power of Pausing

Without the Spirit of God, we can do nothing; we are as ships without wind, or chariots without steeds.

– CHARLES SPURGEON

For as long as she could remember, my friend Sarah had gone to Disneyland every summer with her family. The only place on Earth where you'll wait seventy-five minutes to spin in a teacup, pay nine dollars for a churro, and still somehow feel like it was the best day of your life.

From childhood into adulthood, it was a cherished tradition. But every year, they did the same thing: They rode It's a Small World, bought a churro, watched the parade, and left. She always assumed she had experienced the entire park; it was nice, safe, predictable. It became familiar, even comforting. She told people she loved Disneyland, but deep down, it never felt all that magical.

Then one year, as an adult, Sarah returned with a friend who was a Disney fanatic. But instead of heading to the same old spot, her friend pulled her in a different direction. They zipped past crowds, took secret paths, and suddenly she was standing in front of rides she'd never seen before: rollercoasters, futuristic lands, and immersive adventures. She rode Space Mountain for the first time. She stood speechless in Star Wars: Galaxy's Edge. She laughed harder, screamed louder, and marveled more in one day than she had in decades of visits. By the end of the day, she felt both exhilarated and stunned.

"All this time," she whispered, "It was here and I had no idea."

That's how many Christians relate to the Holy Spirit. They've experienced salvation, but their spiritual journey has been safe, familiar. They've never explored the full wonder and power of the Spirit-filled life. They settle for forgiveness without freedom, presence without power, routine without wonder. But there's more. There has always been more. The Spirit doesn't just offer comfort; He invites you into an adventure, where your prayers have weight, your faith has fire, and your life begins to move with the rhythm of heaven.

However, the kingdom of God isn't a tour; it's more like

a park, and the Spirit is your guide. Don't settle for what's familiar and comfortable.

A Counterintuitive Command

Jesus sent out His disciples to change the world. It was a mission carried out by ordinary people empowered to do extraordinary things. Their call to disciple all nations far exceeded their capacity. So, in addition to commanding them to "go" (Matt. 28:18), He also cautioned them to "wait" for "the promise of the Father" (Acts 1:4), that is, the Spirit.

The disciples needed to pause before they executed their purpose. The key to their success in *going* was in the power of *waiting*. There is power in the pause. While believers today already possess the Spirit, we too need the Spirit's power to do God's work. Carrying out the bold commands of Scripture is too difficult to do in our own strength. We need to wait on God to empower us.

Jesus' instruction to wait might have seemed counterintuitive to His disciples. They had spent three years with Him, having seen His miracles, heard His teachings, and witnessed His resurrection. So why wait?

Jesus' command to wait was rooted in a divine promise. He told them, "I am going to send you what my Father has promised; but stay in the city until you have been clothed with power from on high" (Luke 24:49).

The Spirit's coming had been foretold by the prophets. For example, God said through the prophet Joel, "I will pour out my Spirit on all people" (Joel 2:28). The Spirit would not only be *with* God's people, as He had been in the Old

Testament, but He would now be *within* them (John 14:17). The arrival of God's empowering presence in every believer would mark a turning point in redemptive history.

Power for the mission was in the power of the pause. Jesus was clear: The mission could not move forward without the Spirit. He said, "But you will receive power when the Holy Spirit comes on you; and you will be my witnesses" (Acts 1:8).

The disciples were not merely tasked with passing on information. They were called to proclaim a risen King, stand against hostile cultures, perform signs and wonders, and help establish the church. None of this could be done in human strength. The Holy Spirit would give them boldness, wisdom, words, comfort, discernment, and supernatural courage.

How God Advances the Kingdom

Our dependence on the Spirit is a reflection of Jesus' own ministry. He was anointed with the Spirit to accomplish His mission, because spiritual mission requires spiritual power, a power that comes only through the Holy Spirit. Jesus lived a Spirit-empowered life, and He gives His people that same Holy Spirit so that they can follow in His steps. When we encourage believers to be like Christ but omit telling them about the source of His power, we set them up for an impossible mission.

Jesus made an astonishing claim to His disciples about the Spirit: "It is for your good that I am going away . . . if I go, I will send him to you" (John 16:7). Here Jesus promised that the coming of the Holy Spirit would turn His disciples' weakness into power for mission. The Spirit would guide them into truth, convict the world of sin and righteousness, and glorify Jesus by revealing His heart to them (John 16:8–10). Far from being left alone, they would be empowered with divine clarity, authority, and boldness to carry the gospel to the ends of the earth.

Our need for the Spirit teaches us a vital spiritual lesson: The kingdom does not advance by human impulse but by divine initiative. Relying on the Spirit produces humility. It draws us into prayer. It prepares the heart for God's timing and God's movement. That time of waiting united the disciples in heart and focus. Before they preached or healed in Jesus' name, they were formed in dependence and expectancy.

WE ARE NOT CALLED TO LIVE THE CHRISTIAN LIFE BY EFFORT, TALENT, OR TRADITION, BUT BY THE INDWELLING POWER OF THE HOLY SPIRIT.

I never set out to be a chaplain for an NBA team. Honestly, it wasn't on my radar, my bingo card, or tucked into any five-year strategic plan. The seed was planted in the most ordinary place, a neighborhood pancake house. I was sitting across from two friends: Steve Blake, then suiting up for the Portland Trail Blazers, and Mike Barrett, the team's voice on the broadcast. Between bites of maple-infused German pancakes and scrambled eggs, the idea surfaced almost casually, like a passing comment that somehow lingered. At the time, I didn't think much of it. Life rolled on.

But years later, I found myself standing in a locker room, opening my Bible, and leading my first team chapel. Mike's words echoed in my mind: "This is one of many conversations." Looking back, I see it clearly now: What felt like waiting was really the Spirit setting the pace, preparing me for His timing and His plan.

We are not called to live the Christian life by effort, talent, or tradition, but by the indwelling power of the Holy Spirit. Waiting for and relying on the Spirit is not weakness; it is wisdom. It positions us to receive the fullness of God so that we can walk in the fullness of our calling.

Without relying on the Holy Spirit, we may look busy but remain fruitless. But when we trust the Holy Spirit, we may seem ordinary but become unexplainably fruitful. That leads us to consider what the Spirit's fruit looks like in our lives and in the mission that Christ has given to the church.

Fruit That the World Can't Fake

As we saw earlier in Galatians 5:22–23, Paul outlines the fruit of the Spirit: "love, joy, peace, forbearance, kindness, goodness, faithfulness, gentleness and self-control." These qualities are not just idealistic traits; they are supernatural evidence that Christ is alive within us. They are what the culture longs for but cannot create.

A Spirit-empowered disciple loves sacrificially, not conditionally. They show peace in chaos, joy in trial, and kindness in hostility. When these qualities show up consistently in someone's life, it's not just admirable; it's disruptive. It raises questions. It draws attention. It makes people wonder, *What's different about you?*

The Spirit also produces the fruit of courage and compassion. In Acts 4:31, after the disciples prayed, they were filled with the Spirit and they "spoke the word of God boldly." That boldness didn't come from arrogance or activism. It came from deep conviction born out of divine encounter.

At the same time, the Spirit softens us to see people not as problems but as image bearers of God. We gain Christ's compassion for the lost, the broken, and even our enemies. This blend of truth and grace, courage and kindness, is exactly what our polarized, hostile world can't imitate. It is "the aroma of Christ" (2 Cor. 2:15).

Our culture is hungry for the spiritual but often settles for the counterfeit. New age spirituality, digital self-help, and emotionalism offer fleeting peace but no lasting power. In contrast, the Spirit empowers believers to live in a way that is authentic, holy, and supernatural.

We must remember: The goal of living by the Spirit is not to be impressive or influential in the world's eyes. The goal is to live in a way that is compelling, to make the life of Jesus evident and irresistible. The Holy Spirit doesn't just make us better people; He makes us living temples of God (1 Cor. 3:16), revealing the love, truth, and power of Jesus to a culture in crisis.

Don't Be Foolish

Living by the Spirit is even more imperative when we consider the alternative. The apostle Paul had strong words for believers who tried to follow Jesus in their own strength: "Are you so foolish? After beginning by means of the Spirit, are you now trying to finish by means of the flesh?" (Gal. 3:3).

Paul calls it foolish—not just misguided or immature, but spiritually irrational—to think that the Christian life can be started in the Spirit and then sustained by human effort. From the very beginning, salvation is a work of the Spirit. Jesus told Nicodemus, "No one can enter the kingdom of God unless they are born of water and the Spirit" (John 3:5). The Spirit gives us new birth, new identity, and new desires.

But it doesn't stop there. Just as a baby must breathe to stay alive, a believer must walk in the Spirit to live by faith. Paul reminds the Galatians that they didn't just receive the Spirit in the past; they must continue to be led, filled, and empowered by Him in the present.

Trying to live for Jesus without the Spirit is like trying to drive a car without fuel. You might know where you want to go. You might even have a map and keys. But without power, you're stuck.

The call to live by the Spirit isn't simply a call to "try harder." It's a call to abide deeper. The Spirit doesn't merely help us act like Jesus; He forms Christ within us (Gal. 4:19). Without the Spirit's help, we may appear moral but lack power. We may do religious things but not reflect divine life.

There is a reason so many believers feel burned out: They are trying to do spiritual things without spiritual power. That is not maturity; it is madness. It's like climbing a mountain with no oxygen. When Paul tells us to walk by the Spirit rather than the flesh, he's giving us an invitation. He's saying, "Come back to the source. Don't live like you're alone. Don't fake what only God can form in you."

Spirit vs. Flesh

> **THE CALL TO LIVE BY THE SPIRIT ISN'T SIMPLY A CALL TO TRY HARDER. IT'S A CALL TO ABIDE DEEPER. THE SPIRIT DOESN'T MERELY HELP US ACT LIKE JESUS; HE FORMS CHRIST WITHIN US (GAL. 4:19).**

Of course, living by the Spirit isn't always easy. As we saw previously, our flesh resists the Spirit's work in us. There is a real spiritual battle taking place: "For the flesh desires what is contrary to the Spirit, and the Spirit what is contrary to the flesh. They are in conflict with each other" (Gal. 5:17). This means that effort on our part is required. But this is not self-fueled effort.

Jesus commanded His original disciples, "Watch and pray so that you will not fall into temptation. The spirit is willing, but the flesh is weak" (Matt. 26:41). Likewise, Paul told the church in Galatia, "Whoever sows to please their flesh, from the flesh will reap destruction; whoever sows to please the Spirit, from the Spirit will reap eternal life" (Gal. 6:8). We should actively be living to please the Spirit. The closer I follow the Spirit, meditating on the Scriptures He has inspired and submitting my strengths and weaknesses to His empowerment, the more He does His transforming work in me.

What We Offer to the World

Whether we are living by the Spirit also affects the lives of those around us. We don't just lead people with our words; we lead them with our wells. That is, what fills us will spill over into what we offer others.

If we drink from bitterness, we'll pass along cynicism. If we draw from performance, we'll lead others into striving. If our well is people-pleasing, we'll train others to live for the applause of man. But if we drink deeply from the living water—God's presence, truth, and grace—then what we offer will refresh, heal, and restore.

Thankfully, Jesus offers us more than a distant well. He offers an inner river: "Whoever believes in Me, as Scripture has said, rivers of living water will flow from within them" (John 7:38). John tells us that Jesus was speaking of the Holy Spirit. The Holy Spirit is the river that runs through the soul of every consecrated believer.

When we drink from Him, when we slow down long enough to be still in God's presence, to yield in prayer, to soak in truth, to confess, and to listen, we are not merely refreshing ourselves, we are being filled to overflow. This is more than emotional comfort. This is spiritual vitality.

Spiritual Hydration

It is possible to be a Christian and still live dehydrated. To believe in Jesus but rarely drink from the Spirit. We may settle for church without communion, leadership without intimacy, or morality without presence.

But Jesus invites us deeper, not to sip from shallow religion, but to be immersed in His Spirit, to be flooded with living water from within. This inner river becomes the source of wisdom in our decisions, peace in our chaos, power in our weakness, and love in our relationships.

When I was sixteen, I found myself riding a Greyhound bus alone in the middle of the night. The station was dingy, the kind of place where the vending machine looked like it hadn't worked since the Jackson 5. As the bus pulled out, I wondered who would sit beside me—maybe a kind mom with her child or, knowing my luck, a serial killer. Under the glow of a full moon (which should've been my warning sign), the answer arrived.

At a lonely stop in the middle of nowhere, a man climbed on and dropped into the seat right across the aisle from me. Within minutes he was shouting, cursing, and acting erratic, like a one-man circus nobody paid to see. That's when the guy next to me, who casually mentioned he was ex-military, pulled out a knife and said, "Don't worry, kid, I'll handle it if things get rough."

Suddenly, I realized I was the unwilling referee in a potential midnight cage match. My prayer life went from zero to Pentecostal in about three seconds. I begged God to protect me, to calm the man down, and, most of all, to keep me from becoming a human punching bag. And right there, the Spirit's peace washed over me. Almost instantly, the wild man grew quiet, slumped in his seat, and settled like a tamed lion. I even drifted off to sleep. By the time I woke up, he was gone.

The outworking of the Holy Spirit is often hidden in the fabric of the ordinary, not just in dramatic encounters like that. He is present when a parent chooses patience over anger at the dinner table; when forgiveness is extended after a harsh word; or when courage is found to speak gently in a tense meeting. He whispers wisdom in daily decisions, strengthens us to keep showing up when we feel unseen, and quietly reshapes our character in ways that don't make headlines but change everything.

6

Identity Issues: God Says Who We Are

Religion: "My identity is built on being a good person."

Gospel: "My identity is not built on my record or my performance but on Christ's."

– TIM KELLER

You know those moments in life when time slows down, your palms sweat, and you question every decision that led you to this exact moment? Yeah. That was me on what should've been an uneventful pit stop at a gas station restroom.

As I pushed open the stall door, I heard high-pitched laughter and the unmistakable sound of a woman saying, "These automatic sinks never work!" My stomach dropped faster than a rollercoaster at Six Flags.

I peeked through the crack in the door and saw painted nails, purses, and not a single man in sight. Panic gripped me. I was deep in enemy territory.

My first instinct was to make a run for it, but the coast was never clear. There was always someone freshening up their makeup, chatting with a friend, or teaching a toddler how to aim. I was a hostage in my own bad decision.

Then, plot twist, I heard the familiar sound of my wife entering the stall next to mine. I tried to whisper her name, but she didn't hear me over the sound of toilet paper unraveling like a mummy in fast-forward. So I waited. And waited. I had time to consider every life choice I'd made since kindergarten.

Eventually, I emerged like a ninja. Slipping past the row of sinks, eyes down, praying no one noticed the six-foot-something man with size 13 shoes making an escape. Outside, my family was waiting in the car.

"What took you so long?" they asked.

I explained the whole saga, and they burst into laughter. Apparently, while in the stall next to me, my wife had glanced down and seen my massive shoes and thought, "Wow, that is one tall woman with some serious feet."

We laughed until tears rolled down our cheeks. But here's the spiritual truth I couldn't ignore: I was living out a parable about identity.

I had walked into the wrong space. I didn't belong there. And instead of owning it, I hid. I let fear keep me stuck behind a door, pretending everything was fine, hoping no one noticed. Sound familiar?

Too often, we remain stuck in false identities. We're afraid to be exposed, and we become paralyzed by fear of what people might think. So we try to blend in where we don't belong. All the while, God is whispering, "You were never meant to live like this." We were made for more than hiding in stalls of shame or fear. We were meant to walk boldly in our true identity as sons and daughters of God, even if that means awkwardly owning up to a wrong turn.

So, yeah, I accidentally went into the women's bathroom. But the real mistake? Trying to stay where I didn't belong instead of walking out in truth.

Lesson learned. Identity matters. Also—double check the door sign. Every. Single. Time.

Addressing Identity with Conviction

When it comes to our spiritual identity, we've got to have conviction in what God says about us. Without this conviction, we become identity addicts, chasing likes, roles, and reinventions to feel real. But when we believe God we stop hustling to *become* someone and start living like we *already are* someone—someone chosen, known, and free.

It's one thing to mentally affirm that something is true, but when it comes to what God says about us, we need to have strong convictions. A conviction is something you're willing to die for. A conviction is a belief you hold so strongly that it seems as if it holds you.

Unfortunately, we live in a culture that values feelings over facts. Truth is relative, based on what I feel or think. But the Christian's identity is not based on subjective truth; it's based on the reliability of God's Word and the goodness of His character. This is true even when we don't fully grasp His Word.

I'm reminded of the time when Jesus was with a larger group of His disciples, and a strong disagreement broke out among them. When Jesus told them that life could be found by eating His flesh and drinking His blood, many of His disciples said, "This is a hard teaching. Who can accept it?" (John 6:60). They did not grasp that He was speaking figuratively about believing in Him in light of His impending death. Jesus was aware of their grumbling, and He asked them, "Does this offend you?" (v. 61). Then we read, "From this time many of his disciples turned back and no longer followed him" (v. 66).

Jesus then looked at those remaining and asked, "You do not want to leave too, do you?" (v. 67). Peter responded with these words: "Lord, to whom shall we go? You have the words of eternal life" (v. 68).

This is the kind of conviction we need when it comes to our new identity in Christ.

A New Identity in Christ

The moment you accept Jesus Christ as the Son of God and submit to Him as the Lord of your life, you are instantly, miraculously given new spiritual life. "Therefore, if anyone is in Christ, he is a new creation; old things have passed away; behold, all things have become new" (2 Cor. 5:17 ESV).

To be a new creation in Christ means you aren't just an upgraded version of yourself; your very identity has been transformed. Your old nature has died, and you now live from a radically new identity, an identity defined by Christ's righteousness and empowered by His Spirit.

Our first step toward understanding what it means to be a new creation is asking, "Why is there the need for re-creation?" The need for re-creation is due to the brokenness of the world and the sinfulness of humanity. In the simplest possible terms, the biblical answer to the classic question, "What is God doing about the evil in the world?" is this: He is re-creating the world through Jesus. The more you realize who you truly are and renew your mind with this truth, the more you will see your life and behavior line up with the reality of who you really are in Christ.

In his book *The Reason for God: Belief in an Age of Skepticism,* Tim Keller says, "The Christian gospel is that I am so flawed that Jesus had to die for me, yet I am so loved and valued that Jesus was glad to die for me. This leads to deep humility and deep confidence at the same time. It undermines both swaggering and sniveling."[1]

Distorted and Stolen Identity

Although our identity in Christ is secure through the gospel, Satan likes to distort the truth with his lies. If you've ever been to a wacky house at an amusement park or a fair and looked into one of those crazy mirrors, you know what this is like. The mirrors make you look tall, skinny, wide, or short. That's what Satan does, spiritually speaking.

The result is that we live our lives under a false identity, one that feels shamed, rejected, worthless, despised, or insignificant. But God has given us a different identity in Christ: He declares us loved, worthy, forgiven, accepted, and significant.

True Identity	False Identity
Loved	Shamed
Worthy	Rejected
Forgiven	Worthless
Accepted	Despised
Significant	Insignificant

Here are seven areas in which we tend to live our lives based on a false identity:

- ▷ What I have done (my regrets)
- ▷ What I do (my career/calling)
- ▷ What I have accomplished (my trophies)
- ▷ Who I know (my connections)
- ▷ Who I am attracted to (my sexuality)
- ▷ What I own (my possessions)
- ▷ What I look like (my appearance)

The problem with each of these factors—aside from how exhausting they are—is that they are based on changing conditions and circumstances. Like a buoy in the ocean, they'll cause you to move up and down in your sense of self-worth.

When you focus on your identity in Christ, your faith will grow strong and steady. This means identifying and abandoning any image of yourself that is not from God. Stop accepting what others have said about you, how others have labeled you, and how others have defined you (or what you've told yourself). Instead, start believing what God says about you, knowing that the One who created you is pleased with you for the sake of Christ. That's what defines you.

You are not God's mistake!

Received and Fixed Identity

The modern obsession with constructing identity leads many to live fragmented, performative lives, constantly curating, comparing, and redefining. But in Christ, identity is not something we earn or invent. It is something we receive.

Here's how Paul put it in Colossians 3:3: "For you died, and your life is now hidden with Christ in God." When our identity is rooted in Jesus, we are no longer defined by our past, preferences, performance, or popularity. We are defined by His grace, His righteousness, and His unchanging love. That kind of stability is magnetic in a world built on sand.

The Christian life is based on who we are, not just what we do, meaning God is far more concerned with who we are in Christ than simply what we do for Him. True transformation begins from the inside out, not from external religious actions. God does not save us based on what we have done: "For it is by grace you have been saved, through faith—and this is not from yourselves, it is the gift of God—not by works, so that no one can boast" (Eph. 2:8–9).

Perhaps the most profound verse in the Bible that speaks to our identity is Ephesians 1:13: "And you also were included in Christ when you heard the message of truth, the gospel of your salvation. When you believed, you were marked in him with a seal, the promised Holy Spirit."

When Paul says we are "in Christ" the moment we believe, he is describing a spiritual reality that takes place at the very beginning of our salvation. It is not something we grow into later—it happens instantly when we put our faith in Jesus. The expressions "in Christ" and "in Him" (when referring to Jesus) occur approximately 140 to 150 times in the New Testament.

YOUR IDENTITY IS NO LONGER SINNER, FAILURE, OR OUTSIDER. IT'S SAINT, BELOVED, AND CHILD OF GOD.

To be in Christ is to live from a place of unshakable identity, not defined by what we do, but by what Christ has done. It means we are forgiven, loved, transformed, and sent. This identity frees us to live with confidence, purpose, and joy, knowing that we are fully known and fully secure in Him. Your identity is no longer *sinner, failure,* or *outsider.* It's *saint, beloved,* and *child of God.* That last phrase, "child of God," is worth unpacking.

Adopted Sons and Daughters

Ever since Adam and Eve were alienated from God the Father in the Garden of Eden, an orphan spirit has permeated the earth, causing untold damage! At its core, the orphan spirit is a false identity that leads someone to think they must strive, perform, or prove themselves to be loved or accepted. Whether it's parents, teachers, coaches, friends, coworkers, or anyone else, we naturally want to earn people's approval.

But our penchant for earning paralyzes us before God's offer of true grace. We don't know how to receive favor without working for it. And so, we subtly (or not so subtly) trade away the one true gospel because we prefer to work for and serve God as slaves (or at least as employees) rather than as sons. We don't feel safe letting Him do all the work, and earning gives us some semblance of control. We simply can't believe eternal security and everlasting life could be offered as a gift.

Those with an orphan spirit are constantly trying to push down their sense of alienation, loneliness, and lack of self-worth through constant work, through going from one relationship to the next, or through seeking physical gratification in a life of narcissism and self-indulgence. However, the more they indulge, the more addicted they become and the larger the hole in their heart becomes. Because only the love of the Father can fill a person's deepest emotional needs.

On the other hand, those walking in security as sons and daughters bask in the presence and love of God. They practice the joy of the Lord continually as their source of strength, because they understand that grounding their security and self-worth in anything other than God is like trying to build a house on sinking sand.

Your Worth and Your Value

We hear a great deal today about self-worth, self-esteem, self-image, and learning to love yourself. There is nothing wrong with doing things well for God's glory, for the blessing of others, or for our enjoyment. However, when doing our best becomes the focus, we can become slaves to perfectionism (or to defeatism). Our sense of worth and value becomes warped.

My dad passed away when I was twenty-two years old. He was a pastor and a teacher, but he also loved working on cars. I remember growing up watching him play the grease monkey under the hood fixing up old cars, and I still remember some of the muscle car classics that sat in our driveway. I remember as a young boy crawling beneath the engine, grabbing random wrenches, and pretending to fix something that wasn't even broken. I will never forget all the lessons he taught me about changing the oil, replacing spark plugs, and dialing in the carburetor.

I have great memories of all the sweat and blood, conversations, and nuggets of life wisdom he shared over an oil change. When he passed away, I was given one of his old toolboxes filled with the same mechanic tools we used together. That toolbox is old, dented, and greasy. Most people would likely drop it off at a local Goodwill or garbage dump. But to me, that toolbox is full of memories and sentimentalities. For others its junk. For me, it's treasure. For me, it's priceless.

This is what we call attributed value and worth. Something is valuable because of the worth that someone places on it. In the same way, God attributes value and worth to each of us because Jesus paid the price for us with his sweat and blood. To the world, we may look like ordinary people. Like those rusty old tools, others may see little value in us. But God looks at us and sees a precious treasure.

That's how much value and worth you have. You just have to decide if God's opinion matters the most to you.

Believing God's True Word—Over Jesus and Us

Just prior to going into the wilderness to fast for forty days, Jesus was baptized. At His baptism, it's recorded that the skies opened and the heavenly Father spoke audibly for all to hear, but especially Jesus. "As soon as Jesus was baptized, he went up out of the water. At that moment heaven was opened, and he saw the Spirit of God descending like a dove and alighting on Him. And a voice from heaven said, 'This is my Son, whom I love; with him I am well pleased'" (Matt. 3:16–17).

This is a profound and pivotal moment that reveals the secret to our daily victory. The apostle Peter tells us in 2 Peter 1:17, "He (Jesus) received honor and glory from God the Father when the voice came to him from the Majestic

Glory, saying,'"This is my Son, whom I love; with him, I am well pleased."'

Did you catch that? The moment the Father spoke the blessing over Jesus, He received honor and glory. Most of us don't know how to repel the enemy's lies because we don't know how to receive the Father's truth and blessing over who we are. Many of us have a right theology of God, but we have a bad theology of ourselves. When the Father spoke over Jesus, He received his value, worth, and right identity. When we choose to believe that what God says about us is greater than any other voice seeking to define or distort us, we move from insecurity to in-Christ security.

And yet, many of us wander in the wilderness of a false self, an identity formed by wounds, applause, performance, shame, or comparison. We chase approval, wear masks, and call it strength. But what we call "driven," heaven often calls "orphaned." The false self is not just a psychological struggle; it's a spiritual curse. It's the echo of Eden's lie: "You are not enough unless you become something else." But Jesus came to reverse that curse, not by giving us a role to play, but a name to receive. Sons. Daughters. Beloved.

A Compelling Identity

A secure identity in Christ isn't just comforting for the believer; it's compelling to a world drowning in confusion, insecurity, and performance-based worth. In a culture obsessed with self-definition, constantly shifting labels, and the exhausting pursuit of validation, someone who walks in quiet, grounded confidence, anchored not in achievements or appearance, but in being chosen, forgiven, and loved, is radically countercultural.

THE WORLD DOESN'T NEED MORE IMPRESSIVE PEOPLE; IT NEEDS WHOLE PEOPLE.

When your identity is secure in Christ, you're no longer enslaved to likes, titles, or trends. You're free to love without needing to be loved back. You can serve without needing to be seen. You can stand firm without needing to be understood. That kind of freedom isn't just rare; it's magnetic.

The world doesn't need more impressive people; it needs whole people. People who radiate peace instead of pressure. People who know who they are and Whose they are. When we live from our true identity, rooted in Christ and confirmed by the Spirit, we become a prophetic presence, a living question mark to those around us. "How are they so grounded? So joyful? So unshaken?" And the answer is not self-help, but surrender. It's Jesus. And that is what makes the gospel not only believable, but beautiful.

7

Count the Cost: Loosening the Grip on Self

"He must become greater; I must become less."

– JOHN 3:30

Chained in a dark Roman prison, young Perpetua kissed her infant son for the last time. Refusing to renounce Christ, she stepped into the blood-soaked arena beside her friend Felicity. As wild beasts were released, she stood firm: She was calm, radiant, and unafraid. Mauled, bloodied, and still breathing, she guided the trembling hand of the gladiator to her throat, completing her martyrdom with dignity and resolve. Her death was not marked by fear, but by defiant joy. The crowd fell silent, not in victory, but in awe.

Polycarp, a disciple of the apostle John and bishop of Smyrna, was arrested in his old age and ordered to renounce Christ or be burned alive. His reply is legendary: "Eighty and six years I have served Him, and He has done me no wrong. How can I blaspheme my King who saved me?"[1] As the Roman officials demanded he curse Christ or burn, some who witnessed these events claimed that the rising flames did not burn the elderly bishop. Polycarp stood tall and unwavering. With the crackle of fire rising around him, he lifted his eyes to heaven and prayed aloud. Eyewitnesses said the flames swirled around him like a sail, refusing to touch his body. The smell of burning incense filled the air, not flesh. When the fire failed to consume him, the executioner was ordered to stab him; his blood poured out and extinguished the flames. Even in death, Polycarp was unconquered. His peaceful courage under fire became a blazing testimony that Christ is worth everything.

The stories of Polycarp and Perpetua are powerful because they reveal what happens when ordinary people live with extraordinary faith; faith so real, so rooted in Christ, that they willingly face death rather than deny Him. Their courage under pressure and love for Jesus in the face of martyrdom continue to inspire the church today, even nearly two thousand years later.

The fearless witness of these martyrs exposes the hollow obsession with comfort and self that characterizes many

Christians today, challenging us to take up a cruciform life in a culture addicted to ease, power, and personal gain.

A Cruciform Life in a Culture of Self

For many followers of Jesus today, our death to self likely won't show up in a Roman coliseum, in the midst of flames, or on a literal cross, but it does require a daily rejection of pride and selfish desires. It requires choosing the costly way of the cross to find our true life in Christ. As Jesus Himself said, "If anyone would come after me, let him deny himself and take up his cross daily and follow me" (Luke 9:23 ESV).

In a culture obsessed with self, those who live crucified lives stand out. They are not dominated by the constant pressure to impress, perform, or compete. They carry a quiet confidence, a holy freedom. They are secure, joyful, resilient, compelling. It causes the world to ask, "What do they have that I don't?"

> **WHEN JESUS SAID, "TAKE UP YOUR CROSS," HE WAS NOT BEING POETIC. HE WAS ISSUING A CLEAR WARNING: FOLLOWING ME WILL COST YOU EVERY-THING, INCLUDING YOURSELF.**

That's the power of a life shaped by the cross.

The call to follow Jesus is not a casual invitation. It's not an add-on to an already busy, self-directed life. It is a total, disruptive, transformative summons. And at its center stands something radical and offensive: a cross.

This cross is not a decorative symbol. It's not a tattoo, a necklace, or a bumper sticker. In Jesus' day, it was a death device. It symbolized rejection, humiliation, and suffering. When Jesus said, "Take up your cross," He was not being poetic. He was issuing a clear warning: following Me will cost you everything, including yourself.

A Dangerous Identity

When Jesus spoke His final words before ascending into heaven, He didn't leave His disciples with a safe commission or a comfortable task. Instead, He gave them a dangerous, world-shaking assignment: "But you will receive power when the Holy Spirit comes on you; and you will be my witnesses in Jerusalem, and in all Judea and Samaria, and to the ends of the earth" (Acts 1:8).

At first glance, the word "witnesses" might seem ordinary. It's a word used in courtrooms or testimonies. But in light of the nature of Jesus' mission, being His witness often required more than simply saying some words. For many Christians, including the apostles, being witnesses for Jesus has resulted in persecution, imprisonment, or execution. There's a reason the English word "martyr," which comes from the Greek *martys,* refers to laying down your life.

Jesus didn't promise safety; He promised the Holy Spirit. He didn't say the world would applaud them; He said the Spirit would empower them to endure and proclaim, even to the ends of the earth. This was not a message for the timid, but for those ready to be transformed by divine courage.

In our modern culture, we often want a Christianity that

fits in, doesn't offend, and keeps us comfortable. But Acts 1:8 reminds us that the true gospel creates a courageous witness, not a comfortable one.

To be Christ's witness today still carries risk: the risk of rejection when you speak truth in love; the risk of losing your reputation when you live differently than the crowd; and the risk of ridicule when you stand firm on biblical convictions. Though most of us may not face physical martyrdom, Jesus still calls us to a daily death to self. This includes surrendering our pride, comfort, and control to live lives fully aligned with Him.

Spirit-Empowered Boldness

As we consider the costliness of the mission Jesus has given us, it's important to remember that He didn't simply say to His apostles: "Go be my witnesses." He also told them that they would "receive power" (Acts 1:8). The strength to stand, speak, and suffer as Christ's witness doesn't come from within. It comes from the Holy Spirit.

The Spirit gives us boldness to speak when we're tempted to shrink back. The Spirit gives us words when we don't know what to say. The Spirit gives us peace and endurance when faith is costly. The call to be a witness is not a call to strive harder but to surrender deeper, trusting the Spirit to empower a life of unwavering devotion.

Living as a Modern Martyr

To be a witness today means to live in such a way that your life tells the truth about Jesus, even when it costs you.

It means embodying the gospel in a culture of compromise. It means proclaiming with your choices, relationships, and responses that Jesus is Lord.

Recently, across campuses and stadiums in the US, a new wave of fearless students and athletes is rising, declaring their allegiance to Jesus in ways that turn heads and raise eyebrows. On football fields and in packed arenas, young men and women boldly lift their hands and voices, refusing to hide their faith under the glare of crowds and cameras. Public baptisms ripple through rivers, oceans, and swimming pools, each splash a defiant proclamation that they will follow Christ no matter the cost. In a culture quick to shame, cancel, or mock anyone who stands firm, these moments shine like sparks in the dark—ordinary people risking ridicule to make the gospel known with extraordinary courage.

The early church turned the world upside down because they didn't just believe in Jesus, they belonged to Him, even unto death. Their faith was not private, passive, or polished. It was public and powerful, and people were drawn to its authenticity.

The call to be Christ's witness is still a call to be His martyr. Whether in life or death, our charge is to make Jesus known, not only with our words but with our whole lives. "You will be my witnesses" (Acts 1:8) means you will live, love, speak, and, if necessary, suffer in such a way that the world cannot help but see "Christ in you, the hope of glory" (Col. 1:27). And in a world starving for truth, conviction, and courage, that kind of witness is irresistibly compelling.

The Comfort Culture

We live in a culture that not only pursues comfort; it worships it. Entire industries exist to make life easier, faster, and more convenient. Pain, discomfort, delay, and limitation are considered enemies to avoid at all costs. We curate our lives for efficiency, for aesthetic appeal, and for control. The highest good, we're told, is personal happiness, and the highest evil is personal inconvenience.

But then Jesus comes along with a completely different message: "Whoever wants to be my disciple must deny themselves and take up their cross and follow me" (Matt. 16:24). That message doesn't sell in a comfort-addicted world. Yet it is the very essence of the gospel-shaped life.

Sometimes we casually use the phrase, "It's just my cross to bear," to describe traffic, an annoying coworker, or a tough schedule. But Jesus had something far deeper in mind. The cross represents the death of the self-willed life. It means we no longer live to be served but to serve; we no longer fight for control but surrender to God's leading; and we no longer live for approval, comfort, or applause, but for the glory of Christ alone. This kind of death doesn't usually show up in dramatic moments. It happens in the small, often unseen decisions of daily life.

THE CROSS REPRESENTS THE DEATH OF THE SELF-WILLED LIFE.

Choosing silence when you want to be right. Loving someone who doesn't reciprocate. Practicing self-control in a culture of indulgence. Forgiving someone who's not sorry. Remaining faithful when the crowd drifts. Giving generously when it costs you personally.

Every time we die to pride, lust, greed, fear, or selfish ambition, we carry the cross. Every time we surrender, we are shaped into Christlikeness. And though the world often doesn't understand it, this kind of life compels the world to ask questions.

Why It's So Compelling

Those who live a cruciform life radiate a peace that isn't circumstantial, a love that isn't conditional, and a freedom that isn't performative. This is the kind of Christianity that makes people curious, not just about us, but about our Savior.

Our culture is exhausted by self-focus. The constant pressure to craft an impressive identity leaves people drained and insecure. But the person who has nothing to prove and no image to protect is strikingly free. When we die to self and live to Christ, we become people who don't need applause, status, or control. That kind of peace is striking.

Another reason the crucified life is compelling is that our culture craves authenticity. While social media fuels a performative lifestyle, people are starving for something real. A person who daily dies to pride, image, and ego in order to walk with Jesus carries an authenticity that resonates. They're not playing a role; they're living from a deeper well.

Our culture is also desperate for love with substance. In a world of conditional love and shallow affirmation, self-sacrificing love stands out. Dying to self means loving when it's costly, serving when it's inconvenient, and forgiving when it hurts. That kind of love reflects Christ and draws others in.

The Paradoxes of the Crucified Life

Living the crucified life is a powerful paradox because it flips the values of the world upside down while showcasing the deep truths of the gospel. Consider some of the counterintuitive realities that flow from this kind of life.

Dying is the way to living

"For whoever wants to save their life will lose it, but whoever loses their life for me will find it." (Matt. 16:25). The crucified life seems like a loss: It calls for denying self, carrying a cross, and surrendering control. But this "death" is actually the doorway to real life in Christ. The more we die to sin, pride, ego, and self-rule, the more we come alive to God's joy, peace, and power. It's not the end of freedom; it's the beginning of it.

Weakness is the way to power

Paul said, "When I am weak, then I am strong" (2 Cor. 12:10). In the crucified life, we stop pretending to be strong and start depending on God's strength. As we lay down self-reliance, we receive the sustaining power of the Holy Spirit. Power doesn't come from striving but from surrender.

Suffering produces glory

"We suffer with him in order that we may also be glorified with him" (Rom. 8:17 ESV). While the world avoids pain at all costs, Jesus uses suffering as a tool of transformation. The crucified life means trusting that our trials are not meaningless; they shape us into the image of Christ and prepare us for eternal glory. What looks like loss is actually producing greater gain.

Obscurity leads to greatness

In the crucified life, we don't chase platforms or applause. We serve quietly, love sacrificially, and seek God's glory over our own. Ironically, this humility and integrity often has more impact than any spotlight ever could. Jesus said, "The greatest among you will be your servant" (Matt. 23:11).

Death leads to resurrection

Jesus didn't stay on the cross. He rose. And so will we. The crucified life is not grim or joyless; it's infused with resurrection hope. Every death to self is a seed that springs up into new life, new fruit, new power, and new intimacy with Christ.

The Decision Before Us

Every day, we are faced with a decision: Will I follow the way of the cross, or will I chase the way of comfort? Comfort is easy. It's safe. It costs little. But it cannot transform you.

The cross, on the other hand, is costly. It's painful. It will stretch and break you. But it will form Christ in you.

Jesus never promised His way would be easy, but He did promise it would be worth it. The cross is our compass, and it points us to the kind of life that will endure when comfort fails. A cruciform life, a life shaped by the cross, may not look glamorous, but it is eternally glorious.

8

Radical Character: The Joy of Persevering

Character is formed in the storm, not in the calm.

– CHARLES DICKENS

Thirty years ago, I said "I do" to my beautiful bride. We were young, just finishing college, wide-eyed with dreams of a life spent serving God, raising a family, and growing old together. Like most couples, we repeated the words "in sickness and in health" not realizing those words would become the defining thread of our story.

God blessed us with two incredible children, a son and a daughter. But just after the birth of our second child, my wife, Bernadette, began to develop chronic, unexplained symptoms: nausea, fatigue, migraines, and relentless discomfort. What we thought would be a short trial became a long wilderness. For years, we've pursued answers, doctors, specialists, endless testing, treatments at home and abroad, and healing prayers from the faithful. Yet answers never came. The grief wasn't just about her health; it was about the loss of normal. The normal rhythms of date nights, family vacations, or spontaneous adventures were slowly replaced by a life of managing symptoms, not escaping them.

And yet, this is where God's mysterious work has shined brightest. Through this unrelenting trial, I've watched my wife be shaped into a woman of uncommon depth and radiant character. No sugarcoating—it has been a journey of hope and helplessness, of faith and tears. But Bernadette carries a beauty and a boldness forged only in the fire. There is a surrender in her spirit that disarms people. Even while she lives with daily discomfort, others are drawn to her for comfort. People seek her out not because she hides her pain, but because she embodies a strength and gentleness that makes them believe God is near.

My wife radiates a power that doesn't come from health or ease, but from a God who shapes character in the crucible of suffering. And I can honestly say I have never been more inspired by anyone than I am by her. She is proof that trials don't just test us. They transform us.

The biblical command to "count it pure joy . . . whenever you face trials of many kinds" (James 1:2) can seem like insanity. Yet what if our trials and struggles were recognized as mentors along the journey of our formation and transformation? Not all hardships in life translate into transformation, yet sometimes being mentored by pain can yield its own divine fruit of Christ's character: patience that suffering teaches, compassion that wounds awaken, and resilience that only the cross can forge. Trials sometimes come into our lives in thinly veiled disguises. Our trials are not God's denials. God has allowed the trial, and it is not random. It is a sign of God's approval, not His anger; it is not an obstacle to our growth, but ultimately the fuel for it. Masked behind the chaos is character formation. While these trials might provide momentary setbacks to our visible progress in the faith, they are ultimately providing the fuel we need to get to our destination. They build into our lives passion, perseverance, and deep character change that goes far beyond the surface-level behavior change we usually aim for.

A Gradual Process

As we seek to persevere in the faith, we need to remember that spiritual formation is a gradual process. This is a frustrating reality to our instant-gratification culture; we're used to having the entire world within a swipe of our finger. But the formation of the human soul doesn't work like DoorDash. It is a slow, gradual, and often painful process. If we lose sight of this, we will either grow discouraged and give up, or we will settle for mediocrity.

The Bible has a word for our formational journey: sanctification. To sanctify someone or something is to set that person or thing apart for the use intended by its designer. A golf club is "sanctified" when used to hit a specific yardage. In the theological sense, things are sanctified when they are used for the purpose God intends. A human being is sanctified, therefore, when he or she lives according to God's design and purpose.

Like a child growing up into adulthood, Christians should become more sanctified over time. While there may be occasional setbacks and life-long struggles, God makes His people holy in the long run. The apostle Paul uses himself as an example. He explains that while he is a follower of Jesus, he has not "already arrived" at his goal (Phil. 3:12). He continues to pursue God's call to new life. Being sanctified means embracing weaknesses and trusting in God's undeserved kindness.

Not Our Work

At the same time, formation into the image of Jesus isn't something we do as much as it's something that is done to us by God as we yield to His work of transforming grace. Our job is mostly to make ourselves open and shapable followers to what He is displaying of Himself in these seasons. Pick your analogy from Scripture: We're the sheep, He's the shepherd; we're the clay, He's the potter.

When we unmask the human façade of self-delusion, we realize just how utterly unlike Christ we are in the deepest recesses of our hearts. We are forced to confront our own sins and weaknesses and to see how warped and wounded we really are. In that tender place, we all realize that we need help, and power, from beyond us. We need grace.

FORMATION INTO THE IMAGE OF JESUS ISN'T SOMETHING WE DO AS MUCH AS IT'S SOMETHING THAT IS DONE TO US BY GOD AS WE YIELD TO HIS WORK OF TRANSFORMING GRACE.

This is where Christian spiritual formation moves in a completely different direction from the self-actualization movement or the Western obsession with the project of self. Our society's best vision of transformation is becoming your "authentic self." The focus is inward.

For Christians, on the other hand, the focus should be on Christ. After you establish who you are in Him based on what He has done for you, the next question is, *What does it look like to be conformed to the image of Christ?* Sometimes the answer to that question requires a lesson in humility.

A Mid-Life Lesson

When I turned forty years old, I had a mid-life goal to do something significant to inaugurate my approaching over-the-hill milestone. Instead of choosing a more enjoyable adventure, like a bucket list excursion or a dream golf getaway, I decided to summit a mountain. Mt. Hood, to be more specific. If you drive through the Portland metro area, you cannot miss the picturesque background of Mt. Hood sitting majestically on the horizon.

For over a decade, I had dreamed of climbing Mt Hood and taking that summit picture. The thought of climbing a summit that stares at you every morning was a thrilling prospect. I think my forty-year-old ego was conspiring against my better judgment. As I trained and worked out to get into climbing shape, I mentioned to my wife that my goal was to summit Mt. Hood so that every day as I viewed its glory, it would serve as a visual trophy of something great I had accomplished. A daily reminder of my fading youth.

The hike to the summit was a rush, as we used our ice axes and crampon spikes to scale the glacier wall leading us to the breathtaking beauty of sitting on top of the world. Our group posed and took several photos as we made our mark on its snowy peak. But as they say, "What goes up must come down."

As we began the icy descent, my axe slipped. In a millisecond, I was hurling in a free-fall slide down the side of the glacier ice. I tried everything to slow my fall. All I could do was roll onto my back to prevent a neck-breaking cartwheel down the slope. This maneuver prevented broken bones but did nothing to slow me down. It gave me a clear view of the fast-approaching crevasse that I was on a trajectory to fall into. I was on a direct path toward a death fall deep into the bottomless ice canyon.

Within yards of reaching that cavernous pit, I felt something grab me and bring me to a stop. This goes against all the laws of physics. At the rate of speed I was sliding down the steep slope, my momentum should have continued. As

I came to a full stop, and after the shock wore off, I assessed my body and had no injuries other than a few scrapes.

I instantly knew that God had saved my life. As I limped down the snowy path, a large group of other climbers were passing me on their way up to the summit. They had all just watched me take my fall and bore witness to my impossible arrest. As I passed each climber, they echoed the words, "You're a walking miracle."

On my way down, the Lord and I had a deep conversation, during which I was expressing a ton of gratitude. It was in this conversation that I felt like I heard the Lord speak to me and say, "Son, every time you see this mountain, it will not be a trophy of your accomplishment, but a reminder of My accomplishment in your life."

There are hundreds of days I see that mountain as I drive from my suburban home, so I'm constantly reminded of the lesson in humility I learned that day. I also learned a lesson in spiritual formation.

God invites us to partner with Him in our character formation, but no matter how much we become like Christ, we never get to use His character traits as a trophy for our pride. Becoming like Christ is a miracle, and humility is the path to becoming more like Him.

Learning Our Role

Becoming like Christ is an intentional partnership. We must not only allow God to work His transformation within us but we must also partner with Him in this process. This is not "works righteousness." This is simply obeying what we're told to do in Philippians 2:12–13: "Therefore, my beloved, as you have always obeyed, so now, not only as in my presence but much more in my absence, work out your own salvation with fear and trembling, for it is God who works in you, both to will and to work for his good pleasure."

Partnering with God often means stepping willingly into the fires we would rather avoid. Pain, loss, disappointment, and delay are not detours; they are God's workshops, where the Spirit chisels away our pride, polishes our patience, and engraves His character onto the heart. True partnership doesn't mean we control the outcome or sidestep the suffering; it means showing up, hand in hand with God, surrendering our will to His, and trusting the process. To walk this way is to co-labor with God, allowing the hammer of trial and the fire of refinement to mold, strengthen, and transform us from the inside out.

Seasons of Sanctification

As we think of the process of sanctification, it's helpful to remember that life is made up of seasons. Some seasons are full of joy, celebration, and breakthroughs. Other seasons are heartbreaking and overwhelming. Oftentimes we define who God is by our seasonal circumstances, but part of thriving is being able to recognize what season we are in and having clarity about what God is up to regardless of how we feel about Him.

Having an idea of what God may be up to in a given season can help us to approach it with the right perspective. God teaches us different lessons through different seasons. The chart below can help to identify what season we are currently in and what God might be doing in these moments.

Season of DELIGHT	**Season of DISTANCE**
God seems closer, life is good A Lie: "You have ARRIVED" You offer a GENEROUS faith	God seems distant, life is good A lie: "You are IGNORED" You offer a STEADY faith
Season of DESERT	**Season of DARKNESS**
God seems closer, life is hard A Lie: "You are a FAILURE" You offer a PERSEVERING faith	God seems distant, life is hard A Lie: "You are ABANDONED" You offer a RAW faith

The secret to receiving God's purposes for us through each of these seasons comes down to one word: trust.

Testing Is About Trusting

Let's be honest: Trusting God through hard seasons can feel impossible based on the circumstances of each season. Each season will offer its own specific challenge to remain true to our faith and to trust in the faithfulness of God. In a verse we looked at earlier, notice how the prophet Jeremiah describes the man who trusts in the Lord in the midst of trials:

But blessed is the one who trusts in the LORD,
whose confidence is in him.
They will be like a tree planted by the water
that sends out its roots by the stream.
It does not fear when heat comes;
its leaves are always green.
It has no worries in a year of drought
and never fails to bear fruit." (Jer. 17:7–8)

Jeremiah contrasts a life of faithfulness to God with a life that trusts only in human strength and ability. A way of life that trusts only in human ability is like a shrub that lives in the desert. It is stunted and has no hope for survival for any length of time.

But trees planted by rivers do well. Their soil is fertile, their roots are well supplied with water, and they bear much fruit. Such a tree does not have to "worry" when the heat arises or the drought comes. It is secure because it has a water source that is independent of the weather. So it is with the blessed person. They are graciously planted into a relationship with the Almighty. And whether they experience seasons of much or little, rain or drought, peace or calamity, the fountain of living water continually nourishes them. They will not wither nor be fearful; they will be spiritually prosperous and fruitful.

Life is not predictable. There are ups and downs along the way. When times are good, it can feel easier. But when times feel difficult, it is even more important to trust God. God's unchanging character can give us a firm foundation when things feel unsteady and uncertain.

Life can be going along smoothly for a season. Your job is satisfying. Your friends and family are enjoyable. Your goals, finances, health, and outlook seem bright. Then, all of a sudden, life throws a curveball. Someone you know gets sick. You lose your job. A friend or family member betrays you. The things you felt secure in all of a sudden feel fragile.

How do you trust that God is good in these circumstances? How do you trust Him when you do not understand what is happening? When you cannot see a resolution? These are valid questions, and God wants to help you navigate them.

What Does It Mean to Trust God?

To trust is to believe in the reliability, truth, ability, or strength of something. So when it comes to trusting God, that means believing in His reliability, His Word, His ability, and His character. The Bible says that God cannot lie (Heb. 6:18), that He always keeps His promises (Heb. 10:23), and that He loves you and has good in store for you (Rom. 8:28). Trusting in Him means believing that what He says about Himself, about the world, and about you is true.

Trusting God is not about ignoring your feelings or reality. It is not pretending that everything is okay when it isn't. Trusting God is believing and obeying Him even when it's difficult. Trusting is activated when our believed realm is greater than our perceived reality. Don't let what you perceive outweigh what you believe! Trusting God means letting go of the exhausting need to control every outcome, to figure everything out on our own, and to lean on our own wisdom and understanding. It's stepping off the path of self-reliance and stepping fully into His guidance, just as Proverbs 3:5–6 instructs us: "Trust in the LORD with all your heart, and do not lean on your own understanding. In all your ways acknowledge him, and he will make straight your paths."

If the future feels uncertain right now and worry occupies too much room in your heart, remember this: God is already in all of our tomorrows. He knows our way, and He has a plan. God never asks us to figure it all out on our own. He just asks us to trust Him, to recognize His leadership and purpose in our lives. He promises to make our pathways straight.

Benefits of Trusting God in the Process

When we root our lives by trusting in God, a profound transformation begins to ripple through every part of us. Calmness replaces the chaos of anxiety, and a deep, steady peace settles over our hearts. Strength and resilience rise within us, equipping us to face trials without fear, while clarity of purpose and direction illuminates even the darkest paths. Our emotions find stability, our relationships deepen, and our interactions carry the gentle weight of grace. Spiritually, we draw closer to God, our faith grows richer, and we navigate challenges with confidence rooted not in ourselves, but in Him. In the end, this life lived in His presence leaves us with a sense of contentment, fulfillment, and a quiet joy that no circumstance can shake.

To be clear, trusting God in the process is not always easy. But with intentionality and practice, it can become a regular part of our daily lives. Let's explore some practical steps to cultivate trust in God.

EACH DAY, LEANING ON GOD'S STRENGTH AND GUIDANCE TRANSFORMS THE ORDINARY INTO A SACRED PARTNERSHIP, SHAPING A LIFE THAT MOVES STEADILY IN STEP WITH HIS WILL.

A life surrendered to God begins with intentionally letting go of control and trusting His perfect plan. Develop a strong rhythm of prayer and meditation, seek guidance from spiritual mentors and community, and keep a heart tuned to gratitude by counting daily blessings.

Embrace uncertainty with faith and patience, reflecting on past moments of God's faithfulness as reminders of His unchanging character. Surround yourself with positive, supportive influences, and stay grounded in Scripture. Let go of fear and worry by bringing them to God, allowing His peace to take root (Phil. 4:6–7). Each day, leaning on His strength and guidance transforms the ordinary into a sacred partnership, shaping a life that moves steadily in step with His will.

Desert of Close Encounters

Regardless of how faithful we are, it's inevitable that at times we will find ourselves in deserts. But deserts are not just barren wastelands; they are sacred spaces where distractions are stripped away and the soul is laid bare before

God. In the silence and solitude, we come face to face with our limitations, our fears, and our deepest longings. It's in these dry and difficult seasons that God often speaks the loudest—not with noise, but with presence. Just as He met Moses, Elijah, and Jesus in the wilderness, He meets us there to refine, test, and shape our character.

Your desert might look like an empty house. A hospital room. A counselor's office. A waiting season. A demotion. Or even an unanswered prayer. Regardless, God will not abandon you. Just as He led Israel through the wilderness, and as Jesus Himself was led into the desert to be tempted and tested, the Bible repeatedly shows that these barren, uncomfortable places are not void of God's presence. They are fertile ground for character formation, reliance on Him, and the deepening of faith. The desert becomes both a crucible and a classroom. They aren't detours; they are divine appointments. Don't just ask God *when* you will get out of your desert. Ask Him *what* you will get out of the desert. Sometimes, God speaks loudest where life is hardest.

The Refiner's Fire

In the tapestry of biblical imagery, one powerful and profound metaphor that resonates across the pages of Scripture is that of the refiner's fire. This metaphor highlights God's purifying and transforming work. In the physical realm, metals are subjected to intense heat to remove impurities, leaving behind a pure substance.

Similarly, in the spiritual realm, God, the Refiner, subjects His children to the "fire" of trials and challenges to purify and shape their character. And as the apostle Peter reminds us, this is God's normal way of working in the lives of His people: "Dear friends, do not be surprised at the fiery ordeal that has come on you to test you, as though something strange were happening to you" (1 Peter 4:12).

The refiner's fire serves as a transformative agent, breaking away the impurities of doubt, fear, and complacency, leaving behind a soul refined and strengthened. It's a journey toward becoming more Christlike in our thoughts, actions, and character. But this is a journey that requires grit—spiritual grit.

You won't find the word "grit" in a credible English translation of the Bible. But it's there nonetheless. The Bible's terms for grit are steadfastness, endurance, and perseverance. Grit is the determination to keep moving toward your desired goal despite external challenges and internal weariness. But this biblical grit differs from worldly, "pull yourself up by your bootstraps" grit in a crucial way. Biblical steadfastness and endurance has at its core a faith that rests on the promises of God and is therefore full of hope. True, godly grit is able to strive hard and stand fast because it is empowered by God.

Biblical grit is not a genetic trait. It is an acquired trait, forged in the fires of adversity. That's why the Bible teaches us not to resent adversity, but to be grateful for it.

I think of my friend Cameron, a man whose life was forever changed in a single, heart-stopping moment. He dove into a shallow lake, and the world went dark; he was paralyzed, facing a future he never imagined. The odds were stacked against him, yet somehow, by the grace of God, he survived. The miracle of his life became the foundation for a new mission.

Today, Cameron travels the country in a wheelchair, but his limitations have not dimmed his voice or his impact. In auditoriums, small churches, and community gatherings, he shares the story of Jesus with an authenticity and passion that humbles everyone who listens. His eyes light up as he recounts the moments when God's faithfulness carried him through despair, when the power of Christ became tangible in his weakness.

Watching him move through the world, wheelchair wheels tracing a path of hope, is a lesson in cruciform living. It's a life surrendered to God's purposes, a life that shines brightest in the storm. He embodies the truth that even in brokenness, God's power and glory are revealed. Sometimes the deepest wounds become the most compelling testimony.

A Compelling Kind of Suffering

We live in a time when anxiety is epidemic, cynicism is fashionable, and despair often hides behind success and smiles. In such a climate, few things are more compelling than a person who endures suffering, not with bitterness, but with hope.

The Christian who walks through trials with a heart anchored in God sends a signal to the world. There is a deeper source of strength. There is a reason to hope. There is something more. This is not denial. It is not naïve optimism. It is what the Bible calls a living hope (1 Peter 1:3), a resilient joy that springs from knowing Jesus, not from having an easy life.

People expect anger, numbness, or collapse in the face of suffering. But when believers respond with grace, peace, and even gratitude, it forces a question: *Where does that come from?* It comes from a Savior who suffered first. From the One who said, “In this world you will have trouble. But take heart! I have overcome the world” (John 16:33).

To be sure, biblical hope and joy doesn’t mean plastering on a smile or pretending nothing hurts. Jesus wept. Paul groaned. David lamented. But all of them anchored their faith in God’s promises. That’s why joy is possible, even in heartbreak.

In a weary world, a hopeful Christian shines like a lighthouse in a storm. And it may be that people around you will come closer, not just to see how you endure, but to meet the God who carries you.

9

Fearless Engagement: Don't Be Scared of the World

The Christian life is not about escaping the world but about incarnating Christ within it.

– JOHN STOTT

There's a lie that Christians love to baptize in religious language: "The world is just too far gone."

We retreat behind the walls of our churches, shielding our kids, insulating our comfort, blaming culture for its darkness instead of bringing light to it. We say we want to reach the world, but not if it costs us safety. Not if it gets messy. But the gospel never runs from the mess. It moves in.

A friend of mine, a police officer with Haitian roots, knows this better than most. During the height of protests and riots, our city, Portland, was ground zero for tension. Fires in the streets. Screams in the air. The city didn't just feel divided; it felt flammable. And he was right in the middle of it, carrying the weight of his badge, his skin, and his faith, as well as a family trying to sleep at night.

I remember when he told me he was thinking of leaving. He had a job offer in another state, a safer, less hostile place. And who could blame him? But then came the moment. One night, in prayer, as he poured out all the reasons to go, he sensed the Lord urging him, "Don't leave Nineveh."

Nineveh. That wicked, wild, godless city that God told Jonah to go to, not escape from. It's funny, isn't it? To think of our city as Nineveh. But maybe it's because He still loves Nineveh and sends people to it for its redemption.

My friend stayed. He didn't double down on safety. He doubled down on presence. He chose incarnation. He became the kind of light you can't ignore in the middle of chaos. A calm, steady, Spirit-filled force for peace and truth, standing not *against* the city, but *in* it; for its good, for its people, for the gospel. That's what fearless engagement looks like.

Not shouting from the sidelines. Not building bunkers and blaming the darkness for being dark. It looks like running straight into the fire with love, truth, and power, not because we trust the culture, but because we trust Christ in us.

When we look around at the world, it looks like a dangerous place. It's unjust and cruel, scary and complicated. Our beliefs are regarded as strange, even dangerous. Our instinct can be to retreat to our holy huddle to keep ourselves safe and pure. But Jesus didn't do that. He pressed into the world without being defined by it.

As His followers, we're called to do the same. We can engage our unbelieving neighbors with openness and curiosity. We can befriend sinners while being mindful that God has befriended us. In a world of chaos and confusion, where the lines between good and evil are blurred, we can exercise discernment while loving the people around us.

Living with Urgency in Evil Days

In Ephesians 5:15–16, the apostle Paul writes, "Be very careful, then, how you live—not as unwise but as wise, making the most of every opportunity, because the days are evil." These words carry both a warning and a wake-up call. Paul is urging believers to live with intentionality and spiritual urgency, especially in a world marked by moral confusion and spiritual darkness.

Paul tells us to "make the most of every opportunity," which reminds us that time is not something to kill or coast through; it's a precious, God-given resource to be used wisely. Every moment we're given is a chance to reflect Christ, serve others, share truth, and live in a way that honors our King.

When Paul says, "because the days are evil," he is not being pessimistic. He's being realistic. The early Christians

TO REDEEM THE TIME IS TO LIVE WIDE AWAKE, TO RESIST DISTRACTION, PASSIVITY, AND FEAR.

in Ephesus lived in a culture filled with idolatry, injustice, and immorality. Our time is no different. But instead of retreating, Paul calls the church to step into the brokenness with wisdom, courage, and purpose. Evil days aren't a reason to give up; they're a reason to rise up.

To redeem the time is to live wide awake, to resist distraction, passivity, and fear. It means living each day as a divine opportunity, seeing even mundane moments as sacred ground for kingdom impact. We can't control the times we live in, but we can choose how we live in the time we're given.

Occupy Till I Come: Living with Purpose Until Christ Returns

There is a tension every follower of Jesus must live in, the space between Christ's first coming and His promised return. We have been saved, called, empowered, and sent. But now we wait. And yet, this waiting is not passive. It is not idle. It is not disengaged. Jesus' words in Luke 19, "Occupy till I come," call us into an active, faithful, and purposeful life while we await the return of our King.

When Jesus said, "Occupy till I come" (Luke 19:13 KJV), He was not simply calling His followers to wait. He was commanding them to live with purpose and engage the world faithfully until His return. The phrase comes from the parable of the ten minas, in which a nobleman entrusts his servants with resources and tells them to "do business" until he comes back. The Greek word translated "occupy" captures the idea of actively investing, managing, and carrying out business or other responsibilities.[1] Jesus uses this language to call His people to fruitful and faithful stewardship in every area of life.

In our modern culture, this call is just as relevant, and perhaps even more urgent. The temptation for many believers today is to either retreat from culture in fear or to blend into it without impact. But to "occupy" until Christ returns means neither hiding nor compromising. It means standing firm, working for the advance of God's kingdom, and faithfully stewarding all that He's entrusted to us.

Consider several different aspects of what it means for believers to occupy until Christ comes:

Engage the world, don't escape it

To occupy in today's world means we must engage rather than escape. Jesus did not call His followers to form a holy bubble or wait out the darkness. He called them to be salt and light (Matt. 5:13–16). In a time of cultural confusion, political tension, and spiritual drift, we are called to enter the world as representatives of Christ in business, education, the arts, government, and our homes. We occupy by bringing God's presence into real spaces.

Stewardship, not survival

Occupying also means being faithful with what we've been given. Time, talents, relationships, influence—these are all kingdom resources. God is not just looking for big results; He is looking for faithful servants. Whether you're raising a family, building a business, or attending school, you are called to do it with excellence, purpose, and vision.

In our culture, it's easy to drift into a mindset of survival. Many Christians live as if the goal is to just "hold on" until Jesus returns. But this is not the heart of the gospel. Jesus didn't save us to sit still; He saved us to live as sent ones. We have been entrusted with the gospel, spiritual gifts, opportunities, relationships, and influence. Our calling is not to bury those things in fear or complacency but to invest them in the world for the glory of God. When Jesus returns, He's not looking for what we avoided; He's looking for what we multiplied.

Occupying implies advancing, not merely maintaining. Jesus expects that His followers will take what they've been given and multiply it by making disciples, making disciples, being salt and light in the culture, and bringing life and truth to a broken world. This isn't about striving in our own strength but about walking in the Spirit and participating in God's redemptive work around us.

Faithfulness, not flashiness

In Luke 19, the nobleman returns and rewards thc servants based on how they stewarded what they were given. Not all of them produced the same return; what mattered was their faithfulness. One servant multiplied tenfold. Another five. Both were praised.

In a world obsessed with numbers, followers of Jesus must recover the power of quiet, persistent obedience. You may not be leading a revival, but are you raising your kids in the Lord? You may not be preaching to stadiums, but are you loving your neighbor? You may not be trending online, but are you making disciples?

Occupying is not about being flashy. It's about being faithful with what's in your hands.

Urgency, not complacency

Finally, the phrase "till I come" gives our mission eternal urgency. We don't know when Jesus will return, but we live with the full assurance that He will. That hope fuels our obedience. We are not working for temporary applause but for eternal reward. Jesus said, "Blessed is that servant whom his master will find so doing when he returns" (Luke 12:43). Our lives are to be lived in a state of readiness with an eternal focus.

The Early Church: Distinct and Dangerous to Darkness

When it comes to fearless engagement, the early church once again provides a good example for us. These believers in the book of Acts weren't perfect, but their courage is worth imitating. They caused a compelling disturbance because of their radical allegiance to the way of Jesus. Consider some characteristics that make them worth imitating.

They were treasonous

In Thessalonica, Paul and Silas were accused of "defying Caesar's decrees" for their allegiance to King Jesus (Acts

17:7). In Ephesus, as we saw in a previous chapter, there was a "great disturbance" when Paul threatened idol-making business in the city (Acts 19:23). The unwavering allegiance of Paul and many early Christians to the risen King turned empires upside down, not with violence or power, but with sacrificial love.

They were countercultural

The first Christians stood out in a culture saturated with idolatry, immorality, and injustice. Roman society worshiped many gods, celebrated power and indulgence, and discarded the weak. But the early church did the opposite: They worshiped one God, the risen Christ, at great personal risk (Acts 4:12). They called for repentance and rejected the false gods and idols of their day (Acts 17:16–31). They embraced the poor, sick, and outcast when Roman culture discarded them (Acts 2:45; James 1:27). They practiced sexual purity and marital faithfulness in a society of rampant immorality (1 Thess. 4:3–5). They refused to worship Caesar, calling Jesus "Lord," a title reserved for the emperor. Their lives declared that there is a new King, and His kingdom is not of this world (John 18:36).

They were unified and loving

In a divided and hierarchical world, the church's radical unity across ethnic, gender, and class lines was stunningly subversive. As Paul put it, "There is neither Jew nor Gentile, neither slave nor free, nor is there male and female, for you are all one in Christ Jesus" (Gal. 3:28).

Men and women worshiped together. Masters and slaves broke bread at the same table. Jews and Gentiles were reconciled in Christ. This wasn't just unusual; it was dangerous to the social order.

But it was also a compelling witness. Jesus said, "By this everyone will know that you are my disciples, if you love one another" (John 13:35). And the early church took that seriously. Their sacrificial love for one another, and even for their enemies, deeply challenged a violent and self-centered culture.

They were eternal in their perspective

Perhaps the most dangerous thing about the early church was that many were not afraid to die. They were convinced that Jesus was alive, and that eternity was real. This made them courageous, generous, joyful, and immovable.

They gave away possessions because they knew treasures in heaven were greater. They forgave enemies because they had been forgiven much. They refused to compromise because they feared God more than man. They sang in prison cells because they knew the one in whom they believed.

Their unshakable hope made them uncontrollable by the systems of this world. That's why Rome feared them. That's why darkness opposed them. Because nothing can stop people who have died to themselves and now live for Christ.

What makes a disciple dangerous? A dangerous disciple isn't reckless or violent. They are dangerous to the enemy's schemes, to spiritual apathy, and to cultural compromise.

They pose a threat not because of their power, but because of their complete surrender to Christ. Their lives declare that Jesus is Lord, not just in words, but in the way they live, lead, and love.

Being Dangerous in Today's World

In our current cultural moment, danger looks different, but it is no less necessary. Being a dangerous disciple today might mean loving sacrificially even when it costs, forgiving when it's undeserved, and living a holy life when it's mocked or misunderstood. It means standing firm when others bow down, defending biblical truth in a post-truth world, and refusing to compromise your integrity in business, relationships, or everyday decisions. It looks like choosing contentment when the world celebrates indulgence, being generous in a culture of greed, and creating beauty, community, and hope in the midst of chaos.

TRUE DISCIPLESHIP IN OUR DAY IS RISKY PRECISELY BECAUSE IT DEFIES THE EASY PATH, THE POPULAR OPINION, AND THE CULTURAL CURRENTS, YET IT REFLECTS THE COURAGE AND CHARACTER OF CHRIST IN A WORLD THAT DESPERATELY NEEDS IT.

True discipleship in our day is risky precisely because it defies the easy path, the popular opinion, and the cultural currents, yet it reflects the courage and character of Christ in a world that desperately needs it. It may mean being misunderstood, misrepresented, or even marginalized. But dangerous disciples don't live for applause, they live for allegiance to Christ.

Dangerous and Compelling

Safe faith doesn't change lives. Safe Christianity doesn't confront sin, heal wounds, challenge injustice, or awaken the lost. The world is not looking for polite believers with polished words. The world is desperate for people who actually look like Jesus, people who embody courage, humility, holiness, and compassion. People who live as if the gospel is true.

The kingdom of God is not advanced by spectators or spiritual consumers. It is advanced by disciples who are willing to risk everything because they believe Jesus is worth everything. The early church wasn't perfect, but it was powerful. It was distinct from the world and dangerous to the darkness. And the same Spirit that empowered them lives in us today.

In our own day, the church must recover this kind of gospel courage and clarity. We are not called to blend in or back down. We are called to shine, speak, serve, and stand. The church is most powerful not when it is popular, but when it is pure, united, and surrendered to Jesus.

This kind of light doesn't just expose. It also attracts.

As much as the early church's way of life disturbed those in power, it deeply attracted those who were powerless, broken, and searching. The book of Acts records how "the Lord added to their number daily those who were being saved" (Acts 2:47).

When we stop trying to be safe and start being faithful, perhaps we too will disturb the darkness and draw people to the light. The early church's radical allegiance to Jesus made them dangerous to hell and irresistible to the broken. Their lives disrupted sin, exposed lies, and revealed the glory of a different kind of kingdom, one ruled not by fear, but by grace and truth.

May we follow in their footsteps. May our allegiance to Jesus be so clear, so complete, that the darkness trembles and the world wonders.

10

Radical Community: The Power of Proximity

The most terrible poverty is loneliness, and the feeling of being unloved.

– MOTHER TERESA

Last year, I sat in a circle that should not have existed.

I was in Rwanda, land of rolling hills, vibrant people, and a history soaked in unimaginable bloodshed. In 1994, over the span of just one hundred days, more than 800,000 people were slaughtered in one of the most brutal genocides in modern history. Neighbors turned into executioners. Families were butchered by people they once shared meals with. The scars of that horror still cling to the soil and to the souls who survived it.

And yet, here I was, sitting in a place called Reconciliation Village.

It sounds like a concept ripped from a utopian novel, something idealistic and poetic, but not real. Not after genocide. Not after that kind of evil. But it's real.

In this village, the survivors live side by side with the very people who once tried to erase them. Victims and perpetrators, now neighbors. Now family. I was invited into a circle of such neighbors, and I will never forget what I witnessed.

To my left sat a woman whose eyes carried the weight of hell. She had survived the genocide by hiding in the sewers while her entire family was hunted and killed. I could still sense the silence she had once endured; the cold, the stench, the trauma that refuses to be washed off.

To my right sat a man whose hands were once soaked with blood, her family's blood. He was one of the killers. And now, somehow, unfathomably, they sat together; not in tension, not in fear, but in peace.

I asked the only question that made sense: "How?" The interpreter passed on my words, and without hesitation, they both said the same thing: "Because Jesus forgave us and reconciled us to Himself."

That was it. No theological dissertation. No ten-step recovery process. Just Jesus. The crucified and risen King who absorbed humanity's worst hatred and offered back love. The Jesus who didn't just come to make us nicer people but to create a new kind of people, a kingdom people who live in the kind of community that the world finds absurd.

Reconciliation Village is not a program or a peace treaty. It's a living, breathing, gut-wrenching, gospel-soaked picture of what the church is meant to be: a place where the impossible becomes possible. A community that doesn't just preach forgiveness but embodies it. A people so transformed by the mercy of God that we stop keeping score and start washing feet, even the feet of former enemies.

This is not safe. This is not tidy. But it is compelling. Because only Jesus can build that kind of community.

And if reconciliation can happen there, in the blood-soaked soil of Rwanda, then surely, the church in the West can learn to love across political divides, cultural walls, and personal wounds.

A Different Kind of Community

We were created for this kind of community. The God we worship exists eternally as Father, Son, and Spirit, and the unity and love that exists between the three persons should be reflected in the life of the church. As children of this triune God, we were meant to live in community, with God and with each other. Community is not some peripheral Christian teaching. It is central to the outworking of God's purpose in the world. When we dwell in unity, we rightly image our communal Maker.

Jesus-centric community is meant to be a greenhouse where the Spirit of God can cultivate abundant fruit. Isolation is our kryptonite. We are called to "carry each other's burdens" (Gal. 6:2) as we "encourage and build each other up" (1 Thess. 5:11). The repeated phrase "one another" throughout the Bible speaks to the importance of proximity. In a world divided by politics and ideologies, we are called to express a way of life marked by unity.

> **JESUS-CENTRIC COMMUNITY IS MEANT TO BE A GREENHOUSE WHERE THE SPIRIT OF GOD CAN CULTIVATE ABUNDANT FRUIT.**

When the world looks at the way we do life together as the church, do they see glimpses of heaven? Metaphors describe what the church is like or similar to: light, a flock, a field, or a building. But family is not metaphorical; it is a literal description of what we know of as church. The church is not like family; it is family. This may be one reason the word "disciple," so prevalent in the early part of the New Testament, disappears after the book of Acts.

It is replaced by the terms "brother" and "sister" in the rest of the Bible. Family dominates the self-understanding of the early church. A family that is multiethnic and multigenerational. Our bonds go beyond skin color, income bracket, marital status, and political tribe. As we live out this reality of a spiritual family, we become a model of authenticity, reconciliation, generosity, love, and belonging.

Subversive and Compelling

In a culture saturated with digital noise and starving for real connection, Christian community can be the most subversive and compelling witness. While the world offers curated images and shallow interactions, the church is called to offer something raw, tangible, and deeply human, a place where masks come off, burdens are shared, and presence is prioritized over performance.

In a society plagued by isolation, where people scroll for hours yet feel more alone than ever, a countercultural community of believers who eat together, pray together, grieve and celebrate together becomes a living protest against the loneliness epidemic. The gospel doesn't call us to "like" each other's posts; it calls us to carry each other's crosses. That kind of community isn't just attractive, it's revolutionary.

This kind of radical community is not optional for the believer. It is the evidence of the gospel at work. The early church didn't grow because of strategic plans or powerful platforms, it grew because people saw a community that should not have existed loving one another like family. Jews and Gentiles, rich and poor, men and women, all sharing meals, sharing homes, sharing burdens. They practiced something the modern world is starving for: the power of presence.

Presence over Isolation

Today, we are plagued by proximity without intimacy. We live near people but never with them. Suburban neighborhoods are designed to keep people close enough to wave but far enough to avoid. Churches often mirror this practice with architecture, tightly scheduled services, glossy branding, and plenty of content, but very little connection. We've mistaken convenience for community.

But biblical community isn't always convenient. Nor is it safe and efficient. It's invasive, sacrificial, and sometimes uncomfortable. It requires time, forgiveness, patience, and vulnerability. And it's the most powerful evidence that the message we proclaim is true.

Jesus didn't simply call His disciples into a weekly meeting. He called them into His life. He shared His table, His time, His tears. His strategy for world transformation wasn't mass media, it was meals. His evangelism wasn't just proclamation, it was proximity. He became flesh and dwelt among us. And He calls us to do the same, not just to preach the gospel, but to embody it in radical, relational ways.

To reclaim radical community is to rebel against the isolation of our age. It is to build households of faith, not just ministries. It is to open our homes, not just our church doors. It is to live like the people of God actually belong to each other, because we do.

What the world needs is not another cool church; it needs a compelling community. A people so committed to each other that forgiveness flows freely, meals are shared weekly, and no one suffers alone. A people who understand that proximity is power, because where God's peoplc draw near to one another, God Himself shows up.

Household of Faith

Paul refers to Christians as the "household of God" (Eph. 2:19). In Paul's Greco-Roman context, the word "household," *oikos* in the Greek, refers not just to a physical dwelling but to a family that could stretch beyond common bloodlines. Members of the household enjoyed provision, protection, and a sense of belonging.[1]

In writing to the Ephesian church, Paul uses the same word "household" to capture how the church functions like a spiritual family. In Christ, we no longer live as outsiders, cut off from God, His promises, and His people. Instead, we have been given full citizenship in God's kingdom and welcomed into His family. God is our Father, and we are His sons and daughters. Together we share belonging, intimacy, and inheritance.

Inheritance was passed through families. Land was stewarded by families. Justice, mercy, and generosity were practiced first in the context of family. We see echoes of this in the life of the early church.

The book of Acts describes believers sharing possessions and meeting needs, not through taxation or centralized control, but through relational generosity rooted in a shared identity as the family of God (Acts 2:44–45; 4:32). Paul collects offerings for the Jerusalem church not as a transaction but as a sacred act of solidarity between spiritual siblings (2 Cor. 8–9).

When the church lives as a true spiritual family, it doesn't erase or compete with our individual families but rather complements them with a wider embrace. In God's design, the church is a household of faith where brothers and sisters in Christ care for one another, pray for one another, and meet each other's needs in ways that even natural families sometimes cannot. This spiritual family becomes a place of belonging for the lonely, support for the weary, and encouragement for the discouraged. It is not meant to substitute the beauty and responsibility of our biological homes, but to extend God's love beyond them, so that no one in Christ's body walks alone and every need is met through the shared life of God's household.

The Family of God and a Kingdom Economy

In a world ravaged by fragmentation, economically and relationally, the church is called to be a countercultural economy rooted in spiritual family. We are not spiritual consumers looking for a product; we are siblings in a house where gifts are shared, burdens are carried, and no one is left behind.

To be clear, caring for one another in community doesn't overturn the nation's economic system. We still work jobs, earn paychecks, and live within the flow of the nation's economy. But within the church, a new kind of economy emerges: an economy of grace and generosity. Here, resources aren't just personal possessions but tools entrusted by God to meet the needs of His family. And this includes the most vulnerable among us.

In 1 Timothy 5, Paul gives instructions for how to care for widows, and he bases his instructions on household structures, not state systems. Families were to provide first, and the church would step in when needed. In Galatians 6:10, he writes, "Let us do good to all people, especially to those who belong to the family of believers." This isn't favoritism; it's covenant responsibility.

THE HOUSEHOLD OF GOD LIVES OUT ITS CALLING NOT BY REPLACING THE FAMILIES WE WERE BORN INTO, BUT BY BECOMING THE FAMILY WE ARE BORN AGAIN INTO.

So what does it look like, practically speaking, when the church functions as a spiritual family? It looks like a single mom being served by her small group as they step in to help with childcare, meals, and encouragement when she feels overwhelmed. It looks like an older couple "adopting" college students into their home for Sunday dinners so those who are far from family experience belonging and care. It looks like believers rallying around someone who loses a job by helping with groceries, offering connections, or covering bills until stability returns. It looks like sitting with someone in the hospital so they don't face sickness alone. It looks like families opening their homes during the holidays so no one spends Thanksgiving or Christmas by themselves. It looks like church members showing up with hammers and paintbrushes to help a widow repair her home. This is how the household of God lives out its calling—not by replacing the families we were born into, but by becoming the family we are born *again* into.

Koinonia: More than Fellowship

In many modern expressions of church, we've subtly shifted from this biblical vision to something less human and more corporate. We've traded fellowship for formality, participation for performance, and mutual ministry for professional programming. What makes the church compelling in a disenchanted age isn't our polish, but a people gathered around Jesus, sharing life together in ways the world can't manufacture or market.

This idea of sharing life together and partnering together gets at the biblical concept of fellowship, which comes from the Greek word *koinonia*. Sadly, *koinonia* is often reduced to coffee hour and cookies after service. But biblically, it means far more. It implies communion, mutual participation, shared life, and spiritual partnership. It is relational glue forged not merely by physical proximity but by purpose. It is Christ-centered, Spirit-filled, and mission-oriented. This kind of fellowship is not optional for discipleship; it is the environment in which discipleship happens.

There are over fifty "one another" commands in the New Testament: love one another, bear one another's burdens, confess to one another, encourage one another, serve one another, forgive one another, etc. (see, for example, Rom. 12:9–12). These are not poetic aspirations. They are sacred obligations that require proximity, vulnerability, and consistency.

You can't "one another" from a distance. You can't "one another" through content consumption. You have to show up. You have to stay. You have to risk.

In a culture of hyper-individualism, the church offers a radically different vision, a vision of a people who walk in the light together, stumble forward in grace together, and become more like Jesus together.

The Beauty and Challenge of Real Community

Let's be honest: this kind of community isn't easy. It's disruptive. It gets under your skin and into your schedule. It exposes selfishness and demands grace. But that's exactly the point. We're not called to be comfortable; we're called to Christlikeness. And nothing forms the character of Christ in us like committed relationships with other believers.

Real *koinonia* will stretch you. It will expose the selfishness you hide. It will make you give when you feel empty, forgive when it hurts, and show up when you'd rather run. It is messy. It is loud. It is raw. And it is holy. Welcome to God's household. You will fail. You will hurt. You will forgive. You will be stretched. But you will also see God move.

Come, See, and Belong

Jesus prayed not just for our theology to be correct, but for our unity to be compelling: "That they may be one. . . . Then the world will know that you sent me and have loved them even as you have loved me" (John 17:22–23). Community is not just for the comfort of the church. It's for the conversion of the world.

A fractured world needs to see a unified church. A lonely world needs to see a loving church. A divided world needs to see a reconciling church.

When we live in true fellowship, true *koinonia,* we embody the gospel. We become a foretaste of the kingdom. We show the world what Jesus is like, not just through our sermons, but through our shared lives.

This is the Jesus-centered community the world longs for, and the one you were made for. As Jesus said, "By this everyone will know that you are my disciples, if you love one another" (John 13:35).

Other cultures have strong bonds. Teams, families, and neighborhoods know loyalty. But the church? Our unity is different. It's born in the gospel, fueled by the Spirit, and sealed in love that refuses to quit. When we serve, forgive, and endure together, we create a witness the world cannot copy. We offer living, breathing proof that Christ is real, that grace transforms, and that God's kingdom is unstoppable.

Epilogue

We live in a culture that is drunk on compromise, morally adrift, emotionally exhausted, and spiritually starved. Convictions are traded for convenience, and identity is often built on shifting sand. In this world, a compelling faith doesn't blend in, and it doesn't lash out in anger. It quietly stands out, offering a deeper, truer, more radiant way of being.

But what does a compelling faith actually look like in such a world?

It looks like Jesus.

Not a cliché version of Him, but the one who walked through scandalous towns, spoke to outcasts, challenged religious arrogance, and died with forgiveness on His lips. In a culture of compromise, a compelling Christian is someone who abides in Christ, radiates His character, and resists the pull of spiritual passivity with Spirit-empowered passion.

Our culture swings between two extremes: hollow tolerance or harsh judgment. But a compelling faith threads the needle with grace and truth. It doesn't dilute conviction, nor does it weaponize it. It holds fast to biblical truth, but with a compassionate tone and a humble posture.

Conviction without compassion is cruel. Compassion without conviction is empty. But when both are present, people see something rare: a holy, loving presence that refuses to back down and refuses to push people away. It's magnetic.

It's easy to retreat from the culture. It's also easy to assimilate into it. The harder, holier path is to be present without compromise. Compelling Christians do this beautifully. Like Daniel in Babylon, they live faithfully in the midst of a fallen world without becoming like it.

They don't escape the darkness; they bring light into it. They stay at the table with sinners without adopting the patterns of sin. They resist both isolation and imitation. They live differently, but they stay present. That's what makes them powerful.

People don't just hear the truth from them; they experience it.

What truly separates a compelling Christian is not talent, charisma, or education. It's power—not their own, but the power of the Holy Spirit at work within them. And the difference is unmistakable.

Peace when the world is panicking. Forgiveness when betrayal cuts deep. Boldness when silence would be easier. Joy in the middle of suffering.

In an age of outrage and tribal division, love is often confused with silence or weakness. But a compelling faith is characterized by love.

We are living in a time marked by rapid change. The air is thick with progressive ideals. Culture speaks the language of tolerance, personal truth, and endless self-expression. Yet beneath the surface lies a deep hunger for something more. In this world of blurred lines and shifting values, a compelling faith stands out, not because it is loud or angry, but because it is anchored, vibrant, and holy.

In a world trying to move "beyond" God, the most radical thing a Christian can do is stay anchored to Him. In an age where everything is up for grabs, a faithful, abiding, Spirit-empowered believer becomes a living contradiction—and a living invitation.

Because the most compelling thing in this world is not comfort, relevance, or trendiness . . .

It's a life fully surrendered to Jesus.

Notes

Chapter 1: Contending: Fighting the Good Fight

Epigraph: Jackie Hill Perry, Jude: Contending for the Faith in Today's Culture (Lifeway Christian Resources, 2022), PAGE UNKNOWN.

1. *American Dictionary of the English Language*, s.v. "compromise (*v.*)," https://webstersdictionary1828.com/Dictionary/compromise.
2. David F. Wells, *Losing Our Virtue: Why the Church Must Recover Its Moral Vision* (Wm. B. Eerdmans, 1998), 4. Cited in Trevin Wax, "The Normalization of Slander," The Gospel Coalition, https://www.thegospelcoalition.org/blogs/trevin-wax/normalization-slander/.

Chapter 2: Heart Check: The Real War Behind the Culture War

Epigraph: Dallas Willard, *Renovation of the Heart: Putting on the Character of Christ* (NavPress, 2002), 7.

Chapter 3: Consecration: Purging the Idols from Our Life

Epigraph: John Calvin, Institutes of the Christian Religion, Vol. 1, ed. John T. McNeill (John Knox Press, 2006), 108.

Chapter 4: Beyond Consumption: Feasting on the Goodness of God

Epigraph: A. W. Tozer, *The Pursuit of God* (1948; repr., Moody, 2015), 26.

1. F. W. Danker, et al., *A Greek-English Lexicon of the New Testament and Other Early Christian Literature*, 3rd ed. (University of Chicago Press, 2000), s.v. "μένω," 630–31.

Chapter 5: Increasing Capacity: The Power of Pausing

Epigraph: Charles H. Spurgeon, "A Revival Promise," The Spurgeon Library, https://www.spurgeon.org/resource-library/sermons/a-revival-promise/#flipbook/.

Chapter 6: Identity Issues: God Says Who We Are

Epigraph: Timothy Keller, *Counterfeit Gods: The Empty Promises of Money, Sex, and Power, and the Only Hope That Matters* (Dutton, 2009), 45.

1. Timothy Keller, *The Reason for God: Belief in an Age of Skepticism* (Dutton, 2008), 181.

Chapter 7: Count the Cost: Loosening the Grip on Self

1. "Martyrdom of Polycarp," *Ante-Nicene Fathers, Vol. 1,* eds. Alexander Roberts and James Donaldson (Christian Literature Publishing Co., 1885), 67–69.

Chapter 8: Radical Character: The Joy of Persevering

Epigraph: Charles Dickens, *A Tale of Two Cities,* Project Gutenberg, www.gutenberg.org/ebooks/98.

Chapter 9: Fearless Engagement: Don't Be Scared of the World

Epigraph: John Stott, "The Model: Becoming More Like Christ," cited in Randy Alcorn, "John Stott's Final Message," Eternal Perspective Ministries, 2013, https://www.epm.org/resources/2019/Jan/2/john-stotts-final-message/.

1. "Lexicon: Strong's G4231 *pragmateuomai,*" Blue Letter Bible, https://www.blueletterbible.org/lexicon/g4231/kjv/tr/0-1/.

Chapter 10: Radical Community: The Power of Proximity

Epigraph: Mother Teresa, "Saints Among Us: The Work of Mother Teresa." TIME, December 29, 1975, www.time.com/archive/6878542/saints-among-us-the-work-of-mother-teresa.

1. P. H. Towner, "Households and Household Codes," in *Dictionary of Paul and His Letters,* eds. Gerald Hawthorne, Ralph P. Martin, Daniel G. Reid (InterVarsity Press, 1993), 417–18.